BULLSEYE!

The ultimate guide to achieving your goals

BLAKE BEATTIE

Wrightbooks

First published 2010 by Wrightbooks
an imprint of John Wiley & Sons Australia, Ltd
42 McDougall Street, Milton Qld 4064

Office also in Melbourne

Typeset in Palatino 11.5/16pt

© Blake Beattie 2010

The moral rights of the author have been asserted

National Library of Australia Cataloguing-in-Publication data:

Author:	Beattie, Blake.
Title:	Bullseye: the ultimate guide to achieving your goals / Blake Beattie.
ISBN:	9781742169880 (pbk.)
Notes:	Includes index.
Subjects:	Achievement motivation. Goal (psychology) Self-actualization (psychology) Success.
Dewey Number:	158.1

Cover design by Xou Creative

Printed in China by Printplus Limited

10 9 8 7 6 5 4 3 2 1

Disclaimer
The material in this publication is of the nature of general comment only, and does not represent professional advice. It is not intended to provide specific guidance for particular circumstances and it should not be relied on as the basis for any decision to take action or not take action on any matter which it covers. Readers should obtain professional advice where appropriate, before making any such decision. To the maximum extent permitted by law, the author and publisher disclaim all responsibility and liability to any person, arising directly or indirectly from any person taking or not taking action based upon the information in this publication.

Contents

About the author   *v*

Acknowledgements   *vii*

Introduction   *ix*

1   Dare to dream   1

2   The meaning of life: our lifelong legacy   17

3   What matters most   31

4   POWERTIP: the ultimate goal-achievement system   57

5   The seven saboteurs of success, and how to blast through them   89

6   Habit shift: removing limiting habits   131

7   Implanting goals into your subconscious   153

8   The triple P effectiveness blueprint   169

9   Maintaining momentum: executing the plan   191

10   The magic mindset in goal achievement   207

Conclusion   *227*

Appendix: goal-achievement time line exercise   *231*

Index   *235*

Bullseye! is extremely relevant to anyone wanting to get ahead in life. Why is it that so many people seem to go around in circles not getting to the finish line? Blake has laid out the yellow brick road to success. A book for anyone wanting to go to the next level.

—Guy Leech, World Iron Man Champion

From the first page you know that this book is different—just like Blake. He pulls no punches, he is authentic and he is real. Changing your life by mastering the art of goal setting has never been so relevant and, most importantly, so achievable ... buy this book if you are serious about getting what you want out of life.

—Andrew Griffiths, best-selling author and presenter

Wow, what an opportunity this book brings to anyone reading it. The complete roadmap to achieving success. I would place this book as one of the must reads in 2010 for anyone serious about their future.

—Alan Featherby, Director and CEO,
Rendezvous Hotels and Resorts International

Blake helps individuals identify what they want and then create the momentum and the habits to make them happen!

—Chris Helder, international speaker, author
and CEO, Chris Helder Companies

...a truly captivating book that combines inspirational journeys with easy-to-follow models—you'll be hitting your target in no time.

—Craig Longstaff, General Manager,
Alliance Constructions

About the author

Blake Beattie is the performance engineer. He is an expert at transforming individual and organisational performance through world-class speaking, training and coaching. He builds critical shifts in motivation and work habits that lead to unparalleled performance.

Blake is a director of Inspire Consulting and is the vice chairperson of the Life Changing Experiences Foundation. Through coaching, speaking and training, Blake has provided sustainable long-term solutions to a number of different organisations in Australia, the United States, Canada, Singapore and New Zealand. He is the president of the National Speakers Association of Australia and is also the founder of International Pay it Forward Day, which has seen some amazing random acts of kindness spread to more than 15 countries worldwide.

Blake is recognised as one of the next generation leaders of Australia, having been awarded the Summit Leadership

Award. He has contributed numerous articles on achieving potential to many magazines. Professionals in more than 16 countries read his *Momentum* monthly e-newsletter.

Blake is passionate about transforming performance and making a positive difference with each person or organisation he works with. He is based in Sydney, Australia, and believes he has the best job in the world.

For more information, visit <www.blakebeattie.com>.

Acknowledgements

Bullseye! is the culmination of more than 15 years' work and it wouldn't be possible if it wasn't for the help and support of so many amazing people.

To the organisations I have had the privilege of working with over the past few years: thanks so much for your support. I look forward to continuing to serve you and help your organisation prosper.

To my colleagues at National Speakers, Life Changing Experiences Foundation and Pay it Forward / Random Act of Kindness: you are all champions who continue to make a difference every day. Thanks so much for your support and inspiration.

To my mentors, David Cox, Phil Humby, Doug Malouf and David Weir: thanks for your assistance over the years. It is always appreciated and never forgotten.

To my publishers at Wiley: thanks for your wonderful assistance and believing in this book.

To my literary agent Carolyn Crowther: your work is truly exceptional.

To all my friends: you keep me grounded and focused on what is most important in life. Thanks for everything.

To my family: thanks so much for your love and support. I am lucky to have two of the best parents one could hope for and a wonderful brother and sister. I am truly blessed.

To my beautiful wife Fiona: thank you so much for your love, encouragement and energy. You are a truly amazing person who continues to inspire me each day. I couldn't have done it without you!

And last, but not least, I'd like to thank you the reader. I sincerely hope that this book will make a positive difference in your life.

Introduction

In 1992, a little-known Australian athlete failed to make the semifinals of the Olympic 400 metre race. She was devastated, but determined to turn around the result. Her ultimate goal was to win a gold medal in the Barcelona Olympics in 1996. She worked out that the time she would need to win was 48.6 seconds, so she wrote this number down, and put it on her dressing table, where she would see it every day. She then worked out the time she would need for each of the 400 metre sections and trained accordingly. In 1996, Cathy Freeman ran a time of 48.63 seconds, just three hundredths of a second outside the goal that she had set for herself. She thought the time would be good enough to win gold; instead it was France's Marie Jose Perec who won with an Olympic record of 48.25 seconds. Freeman said that she was happy to get silver because it prepared her for what was to come next: a gold medal in front of her home crowd at the 2000 Sydney games. Success for Cathy came from her singleness of purpose and the clarity of her goal.

For most people, goal setting is something that is done once a year in a tired state on New Year's Day. Countless people make resolutions for the year ahead, such as:

- 'I am going to lose weight this year.'

- 'I am finally going to start a course that will further my career.'

- 'I am going to turn my business around and make my first million.'

- 'I am going to meet my soul mate.'

- 'I am going to save enough money to put a deposit on a house.'

A new year brings a sense of optimism, and with it an opportunity to start again more successfully. It is an exciting time … for a while, anyway.

Fast forward to the end of January. What has happened to the goals you set? Most people's goals have fallen by the wayside. Why? Because time just seems to speed by; other commitments and responsibilities get in the way and old routines and patterns surface, rendering the changes we wanted to make ineffective.

It would be great if there was a way to get back on track and achieve those goals you set in the first place. The achievement system you are about to learn has the potential to do just that. It will transform your performance in all areas of life, and enable you to put past frustrations, disappointments and ineffective habits behind you. You will become more energised as you gain a greater sense of purpose and drive.

A number of years ago I was working at a family resort in Vermont and was asked to play a game of darts with some friends. Not having played darts before, I asked my friends to explain the rules to me: the winner of the game would be the first person who hit each of the target areas in order from one to 20, followed by the bullseye at the centre of the dartboard. I was also told that if you hit a 'double' in the outer ring on the correct number, you would get to skip a number. Similarly, if you hit a 'triple' on the inner ring, you would skip two numbers — a great way to fast track your way to victory. The game rules were simple enough to follow, but my skill level was nowhere near as good as my competition's skill level. I tried to fast track my way towards a win by throwing doubles and triples, but I lacked the accuracy. Not only did I lose the first game, I did not win a game all night. I knew what I had to do, but just didn't have the skills or ability to achieve the desired goal. My competitors had years of experience, so how was I going to compete, anyway?

Think of a dart board for a moment. What is the colour at its centre? All those dart players out there probably know the answer, but for others it may not be clear. Similarly, in life some people are very clear about which targets (or bullseyes) they are aiming for: they know exactly how much they want to weigh; they are clear about the amount of business profit they are gunning for; or they are committed to saving for an end-of-year family ski trip. Other people will not even know where the dart board is, let alone the bullseye at its centre. They are unclear as to what would make them happy in business and in life, or even as to what their definition of success might be.

Just as in dart games there are ways to fast track your success, in life there are also ways to do it in life. These methods can be used to achieve incredible things, and apply equally to all aspects of your life, whether they relate to your work, personal relationships or health and fitness. I am excited about sharing these with you so that you can reach your goals faster. I have known many people who have achieved their goals, only to realise that they were unfulfilled once they reached them. We need to make sure that your goals match your values, and there is a powerful process for achieving this, which I will take you through.

Over the past 12 years, I have had the unique experience of working with thousands of people at all points on the motivation curve. I have worked with top business managers and CEOs, employees at all levels, Olympic athletes, highly disadvantaged teenagers and the long-term unemployed (some of whom had been out of work for more than 20 years). During this time, I read countless books and attended numerous seminars to learn about effective achievement tools that anyone could apply easily and effortlessly.

In the course of my research, I realised that many of the tools on offer had serious flaws. Some of the systems were so complex that the effort required to utilise them was just far too great. Other techniques sounded great in theory, but in practice they delivered very little. I was amazed at how many books on the topic of goal setting and achievement were carbon copies of each other, using the same outdated, regurgitated techniques that failed on a number of different levels.

There had to be a better way: a simple yet powerful system that could deliver results for people regardless of age, background or social status. The system would have to be practical and tick all the critical achievement boxes.

This book is it.

It doesn't matter whether you are a seasoned goal setting professional or someone who is thinking about setting goals for the first time; this book will be of huge benefit to you. If you are already achieving some outstanding results, *Bullseye!* will spur you on to even greater successes. For those of you who have been frustrated because things haven't been going quite to plan, this book will provide you with concrete solutions to get you back on track. If you are relatively new to setting goals (and believe me you are not alone) then you have come to the right place. This book is quite simply a one-stop goal-achievement shop that delivers unparalleled results.

In the first two chapters of *Bullseye!*, you will be inspired by the true stories of ordinary people who dared to dream and achieved their goals against all the odds. Inspiration comes from the Latin word *inspirare*, which means 'to breathe life into'. You will be energised to breathe new life into your goals.

Chapter 3 will take you on a journey of self-discovery to ensure that you know which goals matter most to you, and that you are therefore focusing your energies on achieving things that will make you feel a sense of pride and satisfaction.

Chapter 4 reveals the world's leading goal-achievement system: POWERTIP. The foolproof system will help you formulate each goal correctly to ensure maximum chances of success. POWERTIP is simple to use and incredibly effective, and it will ensure that you are set up for success in everything you do.

Once you have your goals properly formulated, it is important to look ahead to prepare for what could go wrong—otherwise, goal achievement is like trying to compete in a hurdles race where you can't see the hurdles! In chapter 5, I will share with you the top seven success stoppers, and explain what you can do to combat them. After reading this chapter, you will be armed with strategies for getting past any obstacles you may face in the achievement of your goals.

> A bend in the road is not the end of the road unless you fail to make the turn.
>
> —Anonymous

The ability to achieve goals can be hindered by stubborn bad habits, which can be very difficult to break if the right strategies are not in place. Chapter 6 will reveal some powerful techniques that will help break the chains that bind you to bad habits.

In chapter 7, you will learn revolutionary strategies that world-class performers use to embed goals into their subconscious mind. With these strategies, you will no longer question whether or not you will achieve the goals you set; the only question will be: what will you do to celebrate? Together we will break down your goals into achievable steps and then use the time line technique to stimulate the reticular activating system (RAR, the gateway to your subconscious mind). It is a very effective process that you will wish someone had shown you years ago.

In chapter 8, you will discover how to properly map out your goal achievement steps using the triple P effectiveness blueprint. Never before will you have planned and prioritised your tasks with such clarity and purpose. This technique aims to harness three of your most critical resources: time, money and energy. The effectiveness blueprint will give you optimal returns on your investment in each of these three areas as well as giving you a competitive advantage.

In chapter 9, you will discover the secrets to maintaining momentum en route towards your goals using a unique system that is easy to implement. You will learn invaluable strategies to keep you on task and on time towards your goals.

Everything that you will have learnt by this stage in the book will benefit you immensely, but without the right mindset the techniques may prove ineffective. Chapter 10, the 'magic mindset', will enable you to utilise the most powerful supercomputer in the world: your brain. You will discover the important link between thoughts, feelings and actions and how you can shape your goal beliefs towards the outcomes you want. I will show you the practical techniques I wish I had known while going through school—it would have made such a big difference!

Finally, this book will give you the confidence that comes from knowing you have the very best goal achievement tools at your disposal. No matter how good or bad your results have been up until now, I know that I can help you take your performance to the next level. I have been lucky enough to work with some incredible people over the years, and in the process have learnt some powerful lessons. I am excited about sharing what I have learnt with you so that you can achieve the success that you deserve. By reading this book you are one of the few people who 'do' rather than one of the many who 'talk'. Dr Stephen Covey said it this way: 'To know and not to do is not to know'. Therefore, this book is not meant to be passively read, but actively implemented. If you commit to the strategies in this book, there is nothing you cannot achieve. It is a real pleasure to be sharing the journey with you, and I look forward to hearing about your achievements.

Blake Beattie
Sydney
January 2010

Chapter 1

Dare to dream

In 1942, a boy was born into a poor family in a working-class suburb of Glasgow, Scotland. When the boy was four, his father departed for war, and his mother abandoned him. He went to live with his father's two sisters, who treated him badly and continually told him that he was worthless. When his father returned from the military, he sexually abused his son for five years, until the boy was 15.

As a young man, he worked as a boilermaker in the Glasgow shipyards. As a sideline he did some folk singing with a band, where he introduced some comedy into the warm-up part of the act and into the songs. It was here that the man was spotted by a talent scout who urged him into stand-up comedy. From there, he built himself up to be a popular figure on the comedy circuit, working alongside comic greats such as John Cleese. The same man had suffered from Attention Deficit Disorder and been an alcoholic.

Despite his difficult beginnings, he has forgiven his deceased father and moved on; his ability to make the best of a bad situation is something to be admired. He is now a regular face on TV and at comedy festivals, and has long been considered one of the most important comedians of our generation.

From a terribly sad childhood, Billy Connolly overcame adversity and moved onwards and upwards to become a household name—not just within the UK, but around the world. Who would have thought that someone from such humble beginnings could make it that far?

> A poor man is not the one without a cent.
> A poor man is the one without a dream.
>
> —Henry Ford

Think back for a moment to when you were a child. Your whole life was before you, and the possibilities were endless. Your mind had not yet been filled with the restrictions and limitations that other people and life experiences inflict. You were yet to know the meaning of the word 'responsibility', and you were free in body, mind and spirit. What lay ahead was a world full of possibilities, of goals and dreams that were unrealised but never out of reach. The future looked bright. Take a moment to think about what your dreams and aspirations looked like during your early years. What were your hopes and dreams back then?

Fast forward to now. Are you living the dream? Do you consistently hit the targets you aim for? Are you happy when you hit those targets? Are you moving closer to what you want? (Assuming, of course, that you know what that might be!)

Why don't people live the dream?

For many reasons, people are pulled away from what they want most in life. Dreams are rarely actualised overnight, and in this era of instant gratification and short attention spans, it is easy to understand why many people don't achieve their dreams. There are countless reasons why people's dreams are left unfulfilled, but some of the most common ones are:

1 not knowing what the goal is in the first place

2 not having the willpower to commit to a goal

3 not having the discipline to perform the actions required to achieve the goals.

Recently, after delivering a talk in Cairns, I was speaking with a lady who told me how she had always wanted to holiday in Fiji. I was instantly excited for her, because Fiji is a magical place of which I have very fond memories. I asked her when she planned to go, to which she replied: 'If only! I have too many responsibilities here, and we don't have the money for that sort of thing'.

What a shame! This woman had given up on her dream, despite the fact that it was very achievable given some planning and dedication. Many people make excuses for not pursuing their goals, or fail to follow through with actions from time to time. However, saying that something 'can't be done' cuts one off from so many possibilities. We all have myriad reasons for not making certain things happen, but no matter what your background, past experiences, age or current circumstances, you can do so much more than you think you can!

As a teenager, Bill Clinton set himself a goal to become the president of the United States, and to be in office for two terms. At the age of 46, he became the second-youngest person to become president and he was in government for two terms. This clearly demonstrates the power of having a specific goal to aspire to. You may not wish to be president of the United States, but perhaps there is something else you desire above all else.

Without a game plan and a destination to focus on, we can easily get swept away in the business of life. But if you have a dream, by setting goals and taking action, you can turn that dream into reality. You can chart a new course at any time towards a destination of your choosing.

What is truly possible in life?

Is there a life we haven't yet experienced that will deliver us true happiness and fulfilment? Is there a better path than the one we're on, which could take us to new heights of achievement? Could we wake up each morning feeling energised and excited about the day ahead?

In the movie *Dead Poets Society*, Robin Williams's character, Mr Keating, encouraged his students to seek and find their own place in the world rather than just accept a path pre-chosen by parents, teachers or others. One student's father expected his son to go to Harvard Medical School even though his heart was set on becoming an actor. The conflict that ensued is one that many of us face when others expect us to do things that are not in our hearts to do. *Carpe Diem*—'seize the day'—is the film's mantra, and it inspires us to take control of our lives, to live each moment with passion and to begin the journey towards lifelong discovery.

We are all dealt different cards in life, but each individual chooses how he or she plays their hand.

 Blake's TIP Good choices made today create a future you will be proud of tomorrow.

Do you remember anyone at school who was constantly teased by others? One such girl was tormented and teased so much throughout her high school years that she left in her first year. She was thought to have an intellectual disability because she was an undiagnosed dyslexic. Once she left school, things only got worse. An unfortunate set of circumstances saw her become pregnant at the age of 13, and she had a self-administered abortion. She was heavily involved in drugs and proceeded to have a further four abortions during her teenage years. Finally, she admitted herself to a drug rehabilitation centre after watching many friends die from drug use. Not exactly an ideal start to life!

Somehow, the young woman never let go of her dream to be an actress. She managed to become drug free, and she stitched her life back together. You might have seen this lady in films such as *The Color Purple, Ghost* and *Sister Act*. I am referring to Whoopi Goldberg, who says she is where she is today because she 'believes in all possibilities'.

Despite her circumstances, Whoopi dared to dream. Life dealt her a testing hand on many occasions, but she dared to follow her dream and managed to turn things around. She is an example to the world that no matter where you are, or what has gone wrong, the sun will always rise tomorrow. Each new day brings with it hope.

We must all understand that daring to dream does not necessarily hand you success on a platter. Life is, and will always be, full of ups and downs. In fact, you may not always achieve your dreams — despite all your best efforts. But surely the journey, unfettered by doubts or the shackles of fear, is far more fulfilling than no forward journey at all. Surely, if change and challenges are inevitable, you are better walking the path towards your goals than letting them slip away.

One man certainly walked the goal achievement path despite some challenges he faced on the way. From an early age, the person to whom I refer loved music, but didn't enjoy the schooling system. He was an excellent piano player, but quit his piano lessons at the age of 11 because he didn't like practising from a printed page. In high school, he practised so much with his band that he struggled to stay awake at school, and eventually left without graduating. People told him that he would never make money in music, and his mother considered him a failure. By the age of 20, the young man suffered from depression and had even attempted suicide. He then spent three weeks in a psychiatric hospital, which completely changed his outlook. Surrounded by so many people who were seriously ill, the young man decided that he had no right to feel self pity. With renewed enthusiasm, he got a job playing the piano in a bar. It was there that he wrote the autobiographical song 'Piano Man'. This song became a hit, and Billy Joel went on to achieve incredible success in his music career, and as a father and husband.

> You've got to forgive yourself at times and grow from failure instead of letting it destroy you. The thing is never to give up.
>
> —Billy Joel

I hope that you have a true belief that anything is possible, no matter what your personal circumstances may be. These amazing stories of people chasing their dreams regardless of their situation should be a reminder to everyone that there is *always* hope — no matter what the setbacks are — if you dare to dream.

Where do you start?

When it comes to achieving your dreams, there are certain elements that are worth considering. In this next section, I have outlined three areas that play a large role in the manifestation of your goals.

Identify your talents

What are your talents? What are your gifts to the world?

While delivering some talks in high schools a number of years ago, I conducted an activity with some year nine students. I showed the students a large box that was wrapped in colourful paper with a big ribbon tied around it. I then asked the students what I had in my hand. A couple of students guessed what it could be, but finally agreed that they couldn't know for sure what was hidden beneath the wrapping paper.

Of course, the object I was showing to the students was a gift. Without unwrapping it, there was no way to enjoy the contents inside the box. I asked the students if anyone had ever received a Christmas present that they decided not to open. The answer, of course, was no.

Sadly, many people have gifts that they never unwrap. By gifts, I mean unique talents and abilities. It is such a shame when people don't utilise their abilities and share their gifts with the world.

What are *your* gifts? Are you making the most of them? Many people are unaware of their unique strengths, and even those people who are aware of them often under-utilise them.

So how might you uncover your strengths?

During our school years, we often discover that we are naturally more gifted in certain areas. However, many of us have strengths that somehow manage to fly under the radar and therefore are never developed. Unless you try something, you may never know if it can become a strength over time. For example, you might be musically gifted—but if you never pick up an instrument, you will never know. Of course, you can't go around trying everything that crosses your path just because there's a slight chance you'll end up being a prodigy in that field! If you have no interest in music, developing musical talent may not be worth your while.

Here are some suggestions that might help you work out exactly where your true talents lie.

- Ask your family and friends what they think your strengths are.

- Perform an online personality assessment, and see which results resonate most with you. For ideas about how find online personality tests, please visit my website, <www.blakebeattie.com>

- Talk to a professional life coach.

I myself have been guilty of failing to utilise my intrinsic gifts or talents. It wasn't until my second or third year as a professional speaker that I started incorporating accents and character voices into my talks. It is a gift to be able to mimic celebrities such as Arnold Schwarzenegger, Sean Connery and David Attenborough. However, I had not used that gift in front of an audience because of fear— fear that I would look silly; fear that I would fail; fear that maybe my accents were not good enough.

The worst thing about this was that a gnawing frustration grew inside of me because of my refusal to use this skill. This frustration told me that I was not being all that I could be; that I was holding back. I am not alone. Many people hold back and don't use their talents because of fear, and thereby never really try. What a waste!

> **Blake's TIP** Find what you are drawn to. Discover your talents and learn to share them with the world. After all, what's the good of a gift left unopened?

Don't be crippled by fear of failure

> You tried your best and failed miserably.
> The lesson is: never try.
>
> —Homer Simpson

No, I don't subscribe to this advice from Homer Simpson, but you would be surprised at how many people actually share his view.

The late Randy Pausch, a university lecturer who recently lost his fight with cancer, encouraged his students to 'fail spectacularly'. He even offered an award for failing. He encouraged his students to 'go for it', not to hold back and put their best efforts into all their strivings, regardless of the outcome. Pausch believed that mediocrity is everywhere, and that it takes courage and persistence to do great things. It is one thing to dare to dream, but quite another to act on it!

When I was in my final year of high school, I had a friend who studied really hard to get the marks he needed to be accepted into his preferred university course. He would forgo social events to study. I, on the other hand, was focused more on sporting success than academia. I admired my friend's commitment and dedication, but continued to study by means of last-minute cramming. When the final exam marks were released, I somehow managed to get the same exam mark as my friend did, even though he had worked at least three times as hard as I had. Later, it occurred to me that I could have achieved much higher results had I been more committed to my studies.

So, why hadn't I been more committed? Probably immaturity; but I am convinced that it was an element of self-doubt and fear: if I got a low mark, I could always tell people that I hadn't really tried. I had let myself down by not utilising the intelligence I had, and it wasn't until my postgraduate studies that I started achieving the kind of results of which I was capable.

Sadly, many people give up before they even get started. They come up with a host of reasons for which their dreams and goals won't become a reality for them. Others will feel frustration and disappointment when they commit to their goal, but don't reach the heights that they aspire to. If you don't try, commit or persist, then you are pretty much guaranteed to fail.

> You miss 100 per cent of the shots you never take.
>
> —Wayne Gretzky

Never give up

It can sometimes be hard to keep going when setbacks occur. Injury, illness and a host of other circumstances can prevent us from achieving what we set out to. Perhaps, you might have a perfect preparation, but just don't quite hit your target despite your best efforts. During these difficult times, it is our attitude that is challenged and it can take all our strength to remain positive.

We've all heard the saying that winning isn't everything, but try telling that to someone who misses out on winning an Olympic gold medal by two hundredths of a second in the swimming final; or a person who loses corporate sponsorship because he or she only finished 'second' in the world rankings. How about a football coach who gets axed because his team loses too many games? Even though winning might not be everything, losing can be shattering. It can be very frustrating, and even soul-destroying, to miss the mark and obtain results below expectations, especially for someone who has devoted decades of his or her life to a goal.

There are countless examples of exceptional human beings who have risen above their frustrations and disappointments. These people have bounced back from their failures to go on and achieve brilliant results. Their attitude of persistence and graciousness has contributed to an attitude of champions. We can learn from these examples and ensure that we always bounce back from disappointing results with the right attitude.

I could never forget speaking to long-distance Olympic racewalker Jane Saville about her disqualification at the Sydney Olympic Games in 2000 for an 'illegal gait' (a common but unaccepted walking technique). She had a 14-second lead in front of her competitors, and could actually see the podium where she anticipated the thunderous applause from her home crowd as she was awarded the gold medal. Instead, she burst into tears as she saw an adjudicator cross her path to flag her for disqualification—literally seconds before she was to win Olympic gold.

What impressed me most about Jane's attitude to this was the fact that she did not allow her incredible disappointment to leave her bitter. Instead, she said: 'Well, that's my sport. That is the joy and disappointment of sport, particularly the sport of walking'. She could have launched a scathing attack on the judges, but instead she accepted that things don't always go as planned.

Sometimes we win in life, and sometimes we don't. But regardless of the final outcome, the greatest reward is the person we become in the process of trying.

Jane never gave up on her dream of winning an Olympic medal. Despite what happened in front of her home crowd, she won an Olympic medal at the 2004 Athens Olympic Games. It brought tears of joy to her eyes.

By following your dreams, things may not go the way you expect them to. However, it is in these difficult moments that we can discover more about ourselves and learn from the experience.

I think by giving something your very best shot, you should not be left disheartened. It is more when you know you did not put in your best efforts that the pain of regret can and should lead to disappointment.

There are countless other inspiring stories that demonstrate the power of putting in your best effort, but one particular example always stands out in my mind as being extraordinary.

What comes to your mind when you think of a world-class runner? You probably wouldn't think about a 61-year-old potato farmer wearing gumboots, would you? Yet in 1983, a potato farmer called Cliff Young entered the gruelling 875 kilometre Sydney-to-Melbourne ultra marathon wearing overalls and a pair of gumboots. It was thought to be a publicity stunt; that he couldn't be serious about entering, let alone competing against some of the world's top athletes!

Running this race was the equivalent of running more than 20 full marathons back-to-back, but the farmer was determined to compete. After all, he did a lot of running on his farm—sometimes 20 or 30 kilometres in a day; he would sometimes run for two to three days straight to round up his 2000 sheep. He felt sure he was fit enough, so the potato farmer pitted his talents against some of the world's best runners with no formal training, no coach, no proper shoes and, according to many, 'no idea'.

The race began, and immediately the farmer was left behind as the professionals sped past. Those in the race had done the maths and prepared in advance: they would run for 16 hours and sleep for eight hours—this was best practice. However, no-one had told the farmer. He just kept on moving while the others rested. Not only did Cliff Young eventually complete the race but he *won* it! He also smashed the record, shaving almost two days off the existing fastest time and setting a new record time of five days, 15 hours and four minutes.

There was a beautiful twist to this story's ending: Cliff did not even realise that there was a prize of $10 000 for winning the race. He decided to give the whole lot away, $2000 to each of the next five competitors in the race. His reasoning? He 'didn't need much to live on'.

Cliff Young instantly became a national hero. His story was the classic underdog story where no-one believed in his ability to finish the race, let alone win it. He showed the world that anything is possible, and that age, experience and training need not be a barrier. I'd like to think that he also reminded people that money is not everything, and that sometimes the simple things in life are even more important.

Sometimes, no-one may believe that you can succeed. That just makes it that much more special when you prove them wrong.

Many people never receive the awards, trophies and certificates that they deserve, but they maintain a winning attitude by going for their dreams, putting in their best efforts and displaying qualities that others admire.

Dare to dream. Most people set their sights far too low. By believing in yourself and operating outside your comfort zone, you can make a much bigger impact than you ever dreamed possible. Why join the masses who throw small pebbles that barely make a ripple into a large pond? Why not instead throw a boulder in, and make a real splash! Martin Luther King Jr, Mother Teresa, Mohandas Gandhi and Nelson Mandela all had dreams for a better world. But dreaming did not make them great. They took action. Their passion and dedication to their causes didn't just send ripples through the world, but it wasn't their dreaming that made them great. Their actions sent waves of positive energy throughout the world that inspired others to take action as well. Just think how proud Martin Luther King Jr would be today if he could see the first African-American President, Barack Obama, leading the people of the US.

So, learn to think big. There is no point in fearing failure. If you are going to fail, fail spectacularly (you might even win an award for it!). Through both failure and success, you can learn to have a healthy attitude to yourself, to your goals and to the world at large.

> You got a dream, you got to protect it. People can't do something themselves, they want to tell you that you can't do it. You want something? Go get it. Period.
>
> —Will Smith as Chris Gardner in *The Pursuit of Happyness*

Always remember that you don't want your dreams or your life to end up as a long list of excuses. You must set your goals, plan your approach and take action — dreams without action will always be just dreams. In the chapters to come, you will begin to realise that your goals and dreams are within your reach. By setting goals and devising plans to achieve them, you can turn those dreams into reality.

> Today is your day! Your mountain is waiting. So…get on your way.
>
> —Dr Seuss

Chapter 2

The meaning of life: our lifelong legacy

For centuries, people have debated the meaning of life. Diverse and varied theories have been put forward by people ranging from ancient philosophers such as Aristotle, Socrates and Plato, to comedy actors such as the British comedy group Monty Python. Greek philosopher Plato believed the meaning of life was to attain the highest form of knowledge; others believe we choose our values to escape the cognitive reminder of death, known as the terror management theory. Others still believe that life has no meaning at all.

The meaning of life is different for each individual, but many people don't really give it a thought until something goes wrong: sickness; the death of a loved one; or some other life-changing situation occurs. It is in these moments that many people realise that some of the goals they have been working towards are really not that important. Rather than wait for tragedy to strike before we contemplate the meaning of life, we should all aim to build a life that reflects what is most important and set goals accordingly.

> Every man dies; not every man really lives.
>
> —William Wallace, *Braveheart*

The meaning of life

At the end of a person's life, what is the true measure of success? What is the purpose of life? What is a life well lived? Does your life reflect your purpose?

There are an infinite number of answers to the question of what constitutes a meaningful life. It could be about being a good person; making a difference; fame; spiritual enlightenment; reaching your potential; financial wealth; popularity, having the best family life; having the most time; having the courage to be yourself; freedom; loving others; others loving you; life balance; power; living your values; a clear conscience, learning and growing as a person.

Perhaps it's all of these things; perhaps it's none of them.

Typically, books about goal achievement will include a brief section about life purpose at the end of the book. I think that your life purpose and your values should encapsulate everything you do, especially when deciding on which goals to pursue. I have seen far too many people reach their hard-fought goals only to be dissatisfied when they get there. It's like receiving a mouth-watering slice of your favourite cake only to find it tastes of something completely different. What an anticlimax! Other people might love it, but you don't. Just like the cake, certain achievements can look brilliant on the outside, but for one reason or another, they just aren't fulfilling once you reach them. We all have a different lens through which to view the world that is formed by our own experiences. The answer to the question, 'What is a life well lived?' is different for each person.

A friend of mine studied law when he was younger because there had always been an expectation that he would follow in his father's footsteps and become a judge. As he approached the end of his law degree, my friend began to have growing doubts about whether a career in the law was really for him. After five years of studying law, my friend turned around and studied medicine, eventually becoming a practising physician and working for many years with indigenous communities where the pay was meagre. This was a far cry from the wealthy lifestyle he would have enjoyed as a Sydney lawyer. However, he realised this path would never have satisfied him in the way his new career does. He knew that this new path would make his life meaningful and fulfilling, so he changed his goals to reflect his personal values. Those extra five years were needed to realise his true goals, but he found his calling eventually, and it was worth making the change.

Not only does my friend's job make him happy, but it has benefited the numerous communities that he has helped.

> I don't know the key to success, but the key
> to failure is trying to please everybody.
>
> —Bill Cosby

Businesses typically have a mission statement designed to reflect the direction and values of the company. This mission statement enables employees to work together under a common vision, meaning and purpose. There is considerable power in that: each goal they set reflects the mission and purpose of the company. Take, for example, Sony's 1950 mission statement: 'To become the company most known for changing the world-wide poor quality image of Japanese products'. It gave Sony employees a clear direction and focus, and today Sony is one of the leading quality electrical producers in the world.

If successful companies have mission statements, why don't we? By defining and refining a mission statement, we can make better decisions about every aspect of our lives.

> Each morning when I open my eyes I say to myself:
> I, not events, have the power to make me happy
> or unhappy today. I can choose which it shall be.
> Yesterday is dead, tomorrow hasn't arrived yet. I have
> just one day, today, and I'm going to be happy in it.
>
> —Groucho Marx

What is success all about anyway?

Success is about the accomplishment of our aims and purposes. It is the guiding principle that provides us with a sense of direction in key areas of our lives.

If success is about accomplishing our aims, how do we go about deciding what a truly valid goal to aspire to is? To some extent, this can be decided (or conditioned) by the community where we live from an early age. In western societies, the measure of success is often considered in terms of power, beauty, wealth and fame. We often judge one another on the basis of what we earn, what we wear, and where we live. But do these superficial achievements really provide the best framework within which to measure success? Is a widow who devotes her time to assisting disadvantaged families any less successful than a famous celebrity? What about a preschool teacher compared with an accountant? Is a person with chiselled features and stunning abs more intrinsically successful than a plain-looking person? Many people get caught up trying to meet society's collective definition of success, but it may not reflect what is in their hearts.

Angelina Jolie, a noted Hollywood actress, is blessed with striking beauty, celebrity appeal and undoubted acting ability, having won numerous top industry awards including an Oscar. However in 2001, the same year that she won the Oscar, she turned her attention to humanitarian efforts. She joined the United Nations refugee agency and by the end of the same year was named the UNHCR Goodwill Ambassador. She has since visited thousands of refugees in numerous developing countries, donated millions of dollars to charity and has even founded the National Centre for Refugee and Immigrant Children, which provides legal advice to those in need who cannot pay for legal assistance. She has also become a mother six times over (three adopted children, three of her own). For Angelina, success meant more than fame, fortune and beauty. She discovered that part of her purpose was to use her celebrity status to make a difference in the lives of others and she is much more fulfilled as a result.

Indeed, many successful people reach a point in their lives where they need to shift focus from their quest for material wealth to something else. I am not saying that money is the root of all evil, or that money and success are mutually exclusive; I don't believe it is wrong to have a nice house, car or boat. But I do think that sometimes we get caught in a trap of 'keeping up with the Joneses', where we attempt to outdo neighbours, friends and relatives.

A couple I met at a seminar a few years ago seemed to tick all the boxes on the 'societal success list': they were both good looking, had successful careers, celebrity status and a comfortable inner-city lifestyle. Despite all this, they decided to give away everything they owned, including their laptop, car, TV and even both of their well-established businesses. Why? Because they wanted to start afresh — to step outside their comfort zones and spend six months travelling the country to discover the meaning of their life. They called it the 'life changing experiment'.

A timely reality check

After dropping out of university, actor Liam Neeson was working as a fork-lift driver in the Guinness factory in

Northern Ireland when an older colleague told him, 'don't stay here long son, get on with your life'. Neeson realised that his life lacked real meaning and purpose, and decided to do something about it. Today he is a highly respected actor who has appeared in such movies as *Schindler's List*, *Star Wars* and *Love Actually*. He now passes on his colleague's timeless advice to others he finds who are not living their life to the fullest.

> Life is a great big canvas and you should throw all the paint you can onto it.
>
> —Danny Kaye

What Liam Neeson went through is something that many of us experience at some stage in our lives. I refer to it as a reality check.

Daily routines make life easier, but easier is not always better. As much as we need some routine in our lives, we also need a certain amount of variety or else life can become like a walk on a treadmill: the view never changes, and the routine stays the same—same speed, same intensity and same mindset. The repetition is no longer a challenge, and we start to get physically and mentally lazy and unstimulated.

Why does it sometimes feel like we are just going through the motions? Perhaps we have achieved goals that might be impressive to others, but just not to us. Perhaps we feel numb because our core values are not being met.

> Any idiot can face a crisis — it's day-to-day living that wears you out.
>
> —Anton Chekhov

A reality check often occurs when we ignore the signs that things aren't quite right. We sweep problems under the carpet and decide that we can deal with them later. When 'later' arrives, it often arrives via a flood of emotion. In these moments, we have a powerful chance to look at our lives and examine the way we are choosing to live. Sometimes, we realise that we have a mundane and meaningless existence. We feel trapped and locked into a lifestyle that just isn't making us happy.

I remember waiting in the hospital with my brother Clinton just before his big operation. He was about to undergo a dangerous operation that the doctors hoped would remove a malignant brain tumour from somewhere close to his brain stem. My role in the lead-up to the dangerous surgery was to be positive: the family member who inspired and motivated the others, and who believed that Clinton was always going to be okay.

While the doctor talked to our family and Clinton, some of his words really stung me. He was saying, 'There is a good chance of paralysis after this operation, so Clinton may not be able to walk again'. On hearing this, I excused myself for a brief moment, saying that I just needed to go to the bathroom. What I actually did was to go to the waiting room, because I felt physically ill. I blacked out for a few moments. The magnitude of the situation had finally caught up with me, and no amount of positive psychology was going to fix this.

Thankfully, Clinton came through the operation and, years later, he is in remission.

I was reminded of something powerful that day. You never know what is around the corner. Life is precious, and we should always make the most of what we have and be grateful for it. The reality check for me was the decision that I was going to make the most of my time and stop living in fear. I was a shadow of the person I wanted to be, and it was about time that I made the most of the talents and abilities I had been blessed with. It was time to start setting goals in line with my true capabilities.

Sometimes we need to step off the treadmill of life to see and experience life anew. It can be an eye-opening experience. For many, it is a real shake-up—but rather than panicking about our realisation, we should see these moments as great opportunities for much-needed change.

Use reality checks to reassess your goals, or to set new ones. Following are five quick steps that will help you set your goals in the advent of a reality check.

1   Don't panic! Most people have a reality check at some stage in their lives. The thoughts and feelings you're experiencing are vitally important because they can reveal powerful messages.

2   Think about exactly what is not working in your life. Be as specific as possible: if you don't like your job, ask yourself what specifically you don't like about it; if your relationship with your partner

has lost its 'zing', think about the reasons why this might have happened.

3   Reassess your goals or set new ones that reflect your values and life purpose.

4   Decide on the actions you will take to improve your life so as not to repeat the same mistakes and wind up in the same predicament.

5   Act. No, I'm not talking about starring in a Broadway play! The actions you take should enable you to better align your life with your purpose and values.

Some people make regular life adjustments, ensuring their goals match their values. For others, the need for change comes in the form of a defining moment, where one has no choice but to take action. The key is to embrace these defining moments because they provide us with greater insight into who we are and, ultimately, which goals are worth pursuing.

> The ladder of success is best climbed by stepping on the rungs of opportunity.
>
> —Ayn Rand

Defining moments in life

I think there are moments in life that define who we are. It is often in those moments of intense emotion that we see life in new ways. It might be experiencing the loss of a loved one, the frustration of losing your job or the elation of having your first child. These experiences teach us about ourselves and our place in the world. They can wield powerful lessons about what is most important to us, and remind us of how we should be living our lives.

A taxi driver once told me the story of how his life had been turned around by a defining moment. He was involved with the wrong crowd at school and as a result got involved in drugs and some criminal activity. He was hiding behind a tree in the middle of the night when a friend was hauled off by police to jail. Shaken by the incident, the taxi driver made a big decision: he was going to end his dealings with drugs and criminals. Standing up to enemies is never an easy thing, but it can be so much harder to stand up to friends, so his decision to drastically change his life showed tremendous courage. For a long time, the man was friendless. Now he says he is the happiest man in the world. He is married with two children and gets to drive a cab for a living. 'Life is good', is how he expressed it. To be successful, sometimes we need to make important decisions that other people might not like.

> Life isn't about waiting for the storm to pass, but going out there and dancing in the rain.
>
> —Anonymous

The last day legacy

If I were a builder entrusted to construct a house, I would need to know the outcome before I even laid a brick—how many rooms, the layout, placement of windows and so on—and then make plans accordingly. The same applies in life. Begin with the end in mind. What does the ideal end result of a happy, fulfilled life look like? Once you have the vision in place, it is so much easier to plan your goals.

I like to call this next exercise the 'last day legacy', and it is especially good for those who struggle to find the purpose or meaning of their lives. To complete this exercise, imagine that you are looking back on your life in your final days. Answer the following questions:

▫ What kind of person are you?

▫ What do your friends most admire about you?

▫ What do they value most about their relationship with you?

▫ How have you made a difference to them and others?

▫ What achievements are you truly proud of?

▫ What will you be most remembered for?

The magic that lies in the 'last day legacy' is that you turn a mirror back on yourself, reminding you of who you would most like to be. Of course, there are some things on the list (particularly some of your achievements) that you may not have done yet, but completing the exercise will help you see what you'd like to achieve and what you value most in your life. Be creative and adventurous—this exercise is about establishing your hopes and dreams.

> As a well-spent day brings happy sleep, so does a well-spent life bring happy death.
>
> —Leonardo Da Vinci, just days before his death

Having completed the exercise, read what you've written and consider whether you are presently on track to achieving the outcome you'd like. Perhaps your answers will illuminate one or two areas of your life to which you'd like to give more attention.

Discovering the meaning of your life

> *Alice:* Mr Cat, which of these paths should I take?
> *Cheshire Cat:* Well, my dear, where do you want to go?
> *Alice:* I don't suppose it really matters.
> *Cheshire Cat:* Then, my dear, any path will do.
>
> —*Alice in Wonderland*, Lewis Carroll, 1865

Many people are not too dissimilar from Alice: they are not quite sure which way to go in life, and they don't have a specific goal. They often make no choices, and hence get taken along with the current.

By taking the time to work out your life purpose, you will find it easier to choose which goals and decisions are right for you.

If you haven't already written a meaning or life purpose down, I encourage you do so. If you have no idea what your life's purpose might be, don't panic. Just write a list that contains the following information:

- things that you are good at

- things that you enjoy

- things that you wish to succeed at

- what kind of person you really want to be.

To inspire you to do this, I have included some examples from friends and colleagues on my website. Please see <www.blakebeattie.com>.

By living life by your defined purpose, you are able to direct your energy and attention towards a happier, more fulfilled existence by setting your goals in the right direction.

Chapter 3

What matters most

As a society, we live busy and complicated lives. We have more timesaving devices than ever before, but less time. Nearly half of all modern-day marriages end in divorce. One-third of all children are growing up in broken homes. Parents work longer hours, so their children are spending more time in before- and after-school care. People talk via internet chat rooms without saying a word to their neighbour, and important face-to-face conversations are often interrupted by the latest mobile phone ring tone. We are more depressed than ever before, which is demonstrated by the increased use of antidepressant medication over the past decade. We eat copious amounts of fast foods and as a result are more obese. We work longer hours and take fewer holidays. We are very stressed by life, which seems to keep speeding up on us. Many people set and achieve goals, only to feel unfulfilled once their targets have been reached. Life balance is something we may expect to see on the high wire at the circus, but not in our own lives.

So, what is going wrong?

Too many people get caught up trying to succeed in life, but they are never truly happy. The reason is quite simple: the formula for success they are using is all wrong.

If you made a cake and forgot to add the self-raising flour, the finished product would be less than satisfactory. Similarly, if we don't put the right ingredients, in the right amounts, into our lives, it's likely that we will feel dissatisfied with the result. For goals to be worthwhile, they must be aligned with your life's purpose and your deep innermost values.

Just yesterday, I was talking to a man at an event in Sydney about the important job he does as a medical services technician. He works very long hours, and is incredibly committed to his work. I told him how great it was that he was so passionate and dedicated to his profession. He then said something quite profound: 'Yes, but it has come at a cost. My own health has suffered, and working such long hours has caused major problems within my family'. I really felt for this man, as I could see the pain in his eyes. He had worked hard for what he believed in, but suffered in terms of his own life balance as a result. His success had come at too high a price.

Every moment of every day, we are confronted with myriad choices: we get to choose what to think, what to do and ultimately what kind of person we will be. There are so many paths we could take, and trying to choose the right one can be both difficult and stressful. We are constantly confronted with questions such as:

▢ Do I take a job overseas? It's a great business opportunity, but it would mean being away from friends and family for extended periods of time.

▢ I love living in Jervis Bay, but my ideal job is not in Jervis Bay. Should I move to fulfil my work goals or stay to enjoy the sun, surf and lifestyle?

▢ Do I go back to university? It would be hard to study while looking after two children, but I don't want to be a cashier forever.

▢ Do I take the senior position that I've been offered in the company? It pays a lot better, but I will need to work much longer hours as a result.

▢ Do I tell my partner how I really feel about our relationship even though he or she will not like what they hear?

Some decisions are never easy, but having self awareness can make it a relatively painless experience. To better understand this concept, think about a road map for a moment. Have you ever pulled out a map to find directions, only to realise you have no idea where you are located on the map? Guilty as charged! If you don't know where you are, the map is quite useless; but if you know exactly where you are, the map can help point you in the right direction to reach your destination. Similarly, having a clear understanding of where you are in your life will assist you in making better decisions about the future.

The big decisions in our lives can lead us closer to true happiness or further away. Knowing which decision is never easy. I sometimes think it would be great if there were a GPS navigation system inside my brain ensuring that I made the right decisions. I could just plug in my life purpose, together with my top values, and the GPS would provide directions on how to reach my ideal destination. If only it were that easy!

Well, there *is* something that can help steer you in the right direction, and guide you towards the right path: your subconscious mind. It can act like an internal compass if it is fed the right ingredients from your conscious mind. Having a clear awareness of your values enables you to better set meaningful priorities and goals.

Recently, while honeymooning in Santorini, my wife and I got chatting to a lovely Canadian couple, Alexis and Eric. They talked about finishing their business degrees and moving into full-time work. Eric worked for a large American postal service company and had been offered a management position, which he turned down. He explained that there was no way he would sell his soul and work the kind of hours required in management roles, despite the significant pay increase. While others would have leapt at the chance of a promotion, Eric hasn't regretted his decision one bit; he knows that for him, life balance is more important than a bigger pay cheque.

A number of years ago, I received a phone call from a casting agency: they wanted me to audition for the movie

Superman. I had not acted professionally for a few years so the call came quite out of the blue. It was very exciting, so I told everyone about it. My family and friends were all thrilled to hear about the opportunity ... well, all except for one person. My fiancée at the time responded to my excitement with a long pause, followed by a chilling reply: 'I am not marrying an actor'. It was as if someone had hit me with a tonne of bricks. The one person I wanted to support me the most did not. We had been having some difficult times in the lead-up to the wedding, but I realised something important that day: my fiancée loved me more for the person she *wanted* me to be than for who I was.

Being so busy with work, I felt as if I was racing towards a wedding that was making less and less sense. After plenty of talks with my fiancée and counselling sessions to resolve our issues, I made the most difficult decision of my life: I called off the wedding, and subsequently ended the relationship. As painful as it was, it was the right decision. I am now happily married to an amazing woman who loves me unconditionally for the person I am. The old adage from biblical days still makes sense: 'The truth shall set you free'.

The importance of knowing yourself

So, how do you know that you are making the right decisions in life? How can you be sure that the goals you set will make you happy?

The answer lies in the extent to which you know yourself. This is why being connected to your values is so important. You need to know *who* you are and *where* you are (physically, emotionally and spiritually) if you are ever going to be happy and fulfilled.

> Knowing others is intelligence; knowing yourself is true wisdom. Mastering others is strength; mastering yourself is true power.
>
> —Lao Tzu

Have you ever seen a full orchestra playing beautiful, inspiring music? I remember seeing an orchestra perform at the Sydney Opera House when I was younger, and I am still in awe of the way the conductor could command all the instrumental groups to create such a magical sound, despite the different shapes, sizes, and sounds of the individual instruments. He could make soloists shine while the rest blended together in support; he could make the music lift with volume and die down to a bare whisper, while keeping all the instruments in harmony and in time with each other. Each instrument in each section complemented the other, thereby enhancing the overall performance.

I believe the principles that a conductor uses to coordinate the sounds of an orchestra can be applied to our own lives. We must learn to listen to ourselves closely while conducting each area of our lives in a balanced way, because each area of our lives is linked closely with every other area, in the same way that the sounds of the instruments in an orchestra are linked to the overall sound the musicians make. Our health is the backbone that supports all other life areas; our connections with loved ones give us vitality; work and career give us a sense of achievement and purpose; finances provide us with means to take care of ourselves and others; recreation allows us to enjoy our hobbies and relax; and self growth enables us to expand, learn and become better people. By working together, the elements create a beautiful sound that resonates within the very core of our being.

The life-centric wheel of life

The life-centric wheel of life encompasses the important elements of a balanced life. Each area of life is interconnected and dependent on each of the other elements. Even if only one part of the wheel is out of sync, it can have an adverse effect on all other areas. Some examples of this principle are outlined following:

□   If you have poor health, you may lack the energy needed to succeed at work or to connect with those you care about.

□   If you are in a poor financial position, your opportunities for learning and recreation may suffer.

□   If you don't stay mentally fit and learn new skills, your career prospects in an ever-changing work landscape could be adversely affected.

□   If your family unit breaks down, your whole wheel could suffer as a result.

As can be seen from figure 3.1 (overleaf), the wheel consists of five major life areas: mind, body, connection, career and recreation. During your lifetime, the importance you place on each area will shift depending on the life phase that you are in. What was most important to you at the age of 10, for example, might be different from what is important to you now. What was important when you were single might be less important when you have a family. What was important when you first started working might be very different from what you look for in a job, now. Similarly, if you have been retrenched from a job, recently divorced or diagnosed with an illness, your emphasis may shift accordingly.

Figure 3.1: the life-centric wheel of life

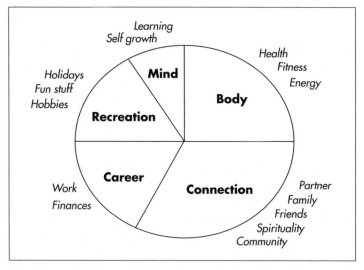

Note: the size of the area allocated to each area of your life indicates how important that area is. It will vary for each one of us depending on age, values and life purpose.

Life balance is about choice. It is about making sure that the things that matter most (your values, which will change over time) are in sync with your priorities: your time, money and energy. Life balance is not about placing equal time and energy in each area of life; it is about the *quality* of the time and energy that you invest in each area of your life for maximum results.

Let's have a look at each important balance area.

Mind (self growth and learning)

Our society is changing rapidly, so it is more crucial than ever before to make a conscious effort to begin the journey towards lifelong learning. According to one British study, the work force of the future will change jobs an average of 19 times, with many people having two different jobs at once. In Australia, experts predict that the majority of children in preschool today will be employed in roles and jobs that don't currently exist.

Our mind is like a muscle — if we don't use it, we lose it. It is critical that we challenge and extend our mind's capabilities so we can better adapt to our rapidly changing world. Learning should be experienced in both personal and professional realms. Our brain loves to learn, and challenging our mind can help stave off health problems such as dementia.

> In times of change learners inherit the Earth; while the learned find themselves beautifully equipped to deal with a world that no longer exists.
>
> —Eric Hoffer

Body (good health and energy)

To get the most out of our lives, we all need to be in peak condition—and this means having plenty of energy. Looking after our health and fitness doesn't just ensure benefits right now, but also later in life. Poor health and fitness, as well as low energy levels, adversely affect all other key life areas, so it is vitally important that we look after our bodies if we are to get the balance right in our wheel of life.

Connection (great relationships)

Our most important needs in life are acceptance and love; companionship and connection are fundamental to our happiness. This connection can present itself in a number of different ways: it can include a connection with a partner, family and friends (pets included); a spiritual connection; or a connection with a community group or other organisation. This sense of being connected is a well-documented key determinant to people's levels of happiness and fulfilment.

Career (satisfying work and solid finances)

We all want to enjoy the perks of life without fear of a financially unsustainable lifestyle. Money is not a bad thing—but the love of money over other things tends to create problems for a balanced life. In order to find satisfaction in our work, we must find a job that we love and that challenges us. In this day and age, we spend too much time working, to hate what we do. If our work is meaningful and fulfilling, even better!

Recreation (hobbies, interests and fun)

Hobbies, interests, holidays and other recreational pursuits help provide us with our zest for life. They enable us to have fun and enjoy the moment, as well as providing us with energy for all other key life areas. Enjoying good holidays each year is important to help recharge our batteries and reinvigorate the body and mind for the year ahead.

Assessing your level of life satisfaction

Using the life-centric assessment wheel (as in figure 3.2), you can assess how you are going in each area of your life right now.

Figure 3.2: the life-centric assessment wheel

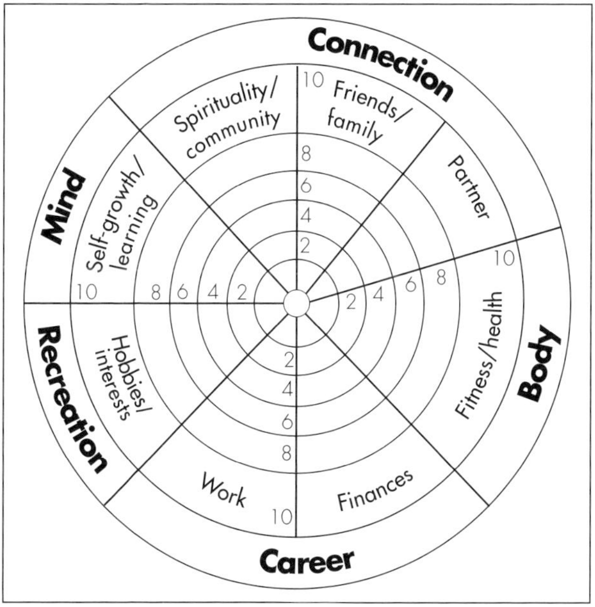

In order to assess how you are tracking in each area of your life, complete the following exercise. Take out a pen, and within each respective area of the wheel, put an asterisk to reflect how satisfied you are at present with that part of your life. For this activity to be beneficial, you must be completely truthful with yourself.

The rating scale is as follows:

2: Completely dissatisfied (it could not be much worse)

4: Dissatisfied (it's not at the level I would like it to be)

6: Somewhat satisfied (it's okay, but things could be better)

8: Very satisfied (I'm quite happy in this area, but there's some room for improvement)

10: Perfectly satisfied (it could not be better; I'm 100 per cent satisfied)

Remember that everyone's life is different, and so are his or her values. So someone who doesn't have a partner may give himself or herself a high score in terms of connection because he or she feels satisfied with being single; similarly, someone else with a partner may give himself or herself a low score because the relationship makes him or her miserable.

Don't fret though if you have some low scores. It is rare to find the life-centric wheel of life in total alignment. Even those who earned a perfect 10 in one area of life often find that such a high score comes at the detriment of other areas. Similarly, if you scored a 10 out of 10 now, you may find it difficult to sustain such a high score all the time. It is important to remember that our life wheels are constantly evolving, as is the correct balance between each of our life areas. Year by year, week by week and day by day, our balance needs to be altered to suit the current circumstances. It's just like walking a tightrope: you are always adjusting and readjusting.

Having completed your rating of each area of your life (as it is for you right now), complete the following steps.

1   Draw lines connecting those asterisks together. Take a close look at the shape of the wheel that is your life right now. If you put that wheel on your car right now, would it be of any use as it is? For some, the wheel might be manageable; but for others, it could use at least a little more air—if not a bit of panel beating!

2   Consider now how your ratings may have changed in each area of your life in the past couple of years. Have they improved or worsened during that time? And what have you done or not done to move your life in that direction?

3   Now for the final exercise for the life-centric assessment wheel—this is the really important part. Take out a new piece of paper and write down in detail how each area of your life would look if you gave each section a perfect 10. In other words, what would it take for you to be 100 per cent satisfied with every part of your life?

As you write down some answers, it might be worthwhile considering the following questions.

◻ Mind

- What would you like to learn?

- Would you like to allocate more time towards growth and development?

- What could you learn that will help you in the future?

◻ Connection

- What would your relationships with family and friends look like?

- What kind of relationship do you want your partner (if applicable)?

- How much quality time would you like to spend with those you care about?

- Do you have regular interaction with social and community groups?

- Are you able to make a difference with a cause or charity?

- What would you like your spiritual connection to be like?

◻ Body

- How fit and flexible would you like to be?

- How well would you like to sleep?

- How good do you want to feel each day when you wake up?

- How much energy do you want to have?

- How much would you like to weigh?

- Would you change your appearance at all? (teeth, grooming, hair, and so on.)

▢ Career

- What would you like to be doing for a job?

- How would your average workday look?

- What sort of hours would you work?

- Where would you be working?

- What kind of people would you work with?

- How much money would you earn each week?

- How would you spend your money?

- Would you donate more money to charities?

- Would you put aside money for family later in life, or would you spend more on them now?

▢ Recreation

- What kind of hobbies, entertainment, sports and holidays might you be involved in?

- Would you travel more often?

- Would you spend more time relaxing?

- Would you go fishing, read more books, play more golf, practise an instrument or join a theatre group?

If you keep these questions in mind while you are describing what your ideal life would look like (where you score

10 out of 10 in terms of satisfaction on each element of the wheel of life), you should be able to produce a thoughtful, inspiring and comprehensive list that helps you to focus your energies correctly, both now and in the future.

Keep writing until you have a really wonderful vision of what a 10 out of 10 life would be for you. Your answers will give you some real insights into what may make you happy in the future.

Shifting out of balance

It is important to realise that sometimes we need to shift out of balance in order to obtain better balance. In other words, there are times when we need to spend more time and energy in one or two life areas to the detriment of other parts of the wheel. Working full-time and studying an MBA part-time left me with little opportunity to balance out important areas of my life. On my life-centric assessment wheel, my recreation score dropped to about a four out of 10 for a while, as I found it difficult to find time to spend with family and friends. However, this was a sacrifice I was willing to make, as it would enable me to improve two other life areas in the long term, specifically the mind and career areas.

Having said that, it's important to understand the difference between healthy and unhealthy phases of being out of balance. Sometimes, small sacrifices to your balance can make you happier and more fulfilled in the future.

When moving out of balance, there is one vitally important thing to remember: always keep an eye on how the rest of the wheel is going, and put the necessary effort into restoring the wheel to a more balanced state as soon as possible. I cannot stress enough how important this is, because I have seen the irreversible damage it has done when someone has remained out of balance for too long. In table 3.1 I have listed some of the comments that I have heard during one-on-one discussions with clients.

Table 3.1: unbalanced wheel of life caused by neglected life areas

Comment	Neglected life areas
I was only trying to provide a great life for my family. Yes, I worked long hours — but someone had to pay the bills. (Senior manager for a large transport company. His wife was filing for divorce.)	Health Connection Recreation
I play online computer games for roughly 14 hours a day. (Unemployed father of two who had been out of work for three years.)	Career Finances Health Mind Connection
I know that my cholesterol is high and that I shouldn't drink and smoke as much as I do. But hey, you only live once. (Assistant manager for a large retail store. Cholesterol reading was at a dangerous level. His father and grandfather had both died of heart attacks.)	Health

I'm sure you know of people who have let their lives get out of balance for too long and have paid the price. This happens far more often than I would like to admit, especially considering the breakneck speed at which we tend to live our lives. In each case, people's priorities haven't matched their values.

The importance of matching values with priorities is an important one, which will be discussed in the following section.

Values versus priorities

Often it takes a life-changing experience—such as an illness or the loss of a loved one—for us to get back in touch with our core values. But why wait for something bad to happen to get into alignment? Why not start re-aligning your goals and priorities with your key values right now? Getting the balance right is not always easy, but it is an important component of our happiness. I distinguish between values and priorities as follows.

Values: what matters most in your life. These are the things that you consider to be the most important parts of your life. If they were taken away, you would feel empty inside. Examples include family; friends; health; spiritual connection; finances; certain possessions; career; community involvement; hobbies; and recreational pur-suits. The relative importance of each area may change with age and changing personal circumstances.

 Blake's TIP If values are the framework in the house of life, then your priorities are the building blocks.

Priorities: where you choose to spend your time, money and energy each day. One of the greatest powers we possess is the power to choose. We get to choose what to spend our money on, how to distribute our time and where to expend our valuable energy. However, there is always an opportunity cost involved, whereby spending in one area means you forego possible spending in another area.

> Most people fail in life because they major in minor things.
>
> —Anthony Robbins

Unhappy people tend to have the balance all wrong. They spend far too much time, money and energy on areas of their lives that give them little genuine satisfaction. A perfect example is the insatiable thirst that some people have for material possessions. The thirst rarely goes away as possessions fill the void only for a fleeting moment. In these situations, a core value is not being met, and the lust for new possessions is merely a substitute for something more significant.

Awareness of the problem is the first step towards balancing values, priorities and goals. It is like being on a runaway train hurtling towards a less-than-ideal destination: hopping off that train to ensure it is taking you in the right direction is always a wise move. That way you can change platforms (or directions) to ensure you are heading towards a happier destination.

Align your core values with your key priorities

So, how do you go about ensuring that your values and your priorities are in harmony?

Following is a quick exercise that will help you discover whether or not your values align with your priorities.

The first step is to identify what is most important to you by writing a list of your top values. Look at the life-centric wheel of life on page 38 and think carefully about what is most important to you at this stage in your life. In the left-hand column of table 3.2, write down your top value areas in order from most important to least important. Perhaps you could call your list, 'The six values that matter most to me'.

Table 3.2: top six most important values

Value area	What your value area means to you

Following is an example of a list of values that a good friend of mine came up with.

1   *Family:* having a loving and supportive family life.
2   *Fitness and health:* being physically strong, flexible and energetic
3   *Paying off the mortgage:* becoming debt free within 10 years
4   *Holidays:* taking four full weeks of holidays with the family each year
5   *Career:* increasing skills and getting a promotion
6   *Friends:* making quality time for close friends.

The second step is to look at the way in which you currently prioritise the scarce resources you have at your disposal. We all have limited time, money and energy and the trick is to spend them in a way that reflects our values.

For example, I remember meeting one man who couldn't afford a gym membership, but would spend more than a hundred dollars on cigarettes and alcohol consumption on a Saturday night. The value he placed on his health was higher than the value he placed on recreation, but his priorities did not reflect this.

Similarly, a friend told me that her most important value was to find a life partner. She wanted to have children, and was aware that her biological clock was ticking. My friend had absolute clarity on what she wanted. However, it was clear that her priorities did not even come close to matching her values. She worked 80 hour weeks in a high-powered executive position, and was often too tired to go out when she did have spare time. Her work goals were in direct conflict with her personal goals, which led to growing dissatisfaction.

Think about the amount of time, money and energy you spent in each value area over the past month. Based on your answer, decide if it was a low, medium or high priority. For example, if I went to to the gym five times a week and ate healthily, I might decide that I made health a 'high' priority based on my allocations over the past month.

If you find that your highest value areas are not a high priority, you need to ask yourself why. Your values may have changed, or you may recognise the need to go out of balance for a short period of time to get better balance. Generally, the discrepancy between values and priorities occurs because we just don't have the balance right. The key is to make changes to get back into better balance sooner rather than later, and make a commitment to changing your allocations based on what matters most.

Table 3.3: relationship between values and priorities in the past month

Value area	How much of a priority are you making this value area at the moment?*		
	Low	Medium	High

*Base your answers on where you allocated your limited time, money and energy over the past month.

The third step is to take action. For example, if you know you aren't spending enough time with the family, check your diary and reorganise your timetable so that you have definite periods of quality time with the family. If you are not saving enough money to get out of debt, perhaps there are ways you can better manage your money.

Reassess your values and priorities on a monthly basis to ensure that your priorities match your values. By keeping track of your progress in each area of your life on a regular basis, you are better able to maintain balance. It will help ensure that your goals, values and priorities are all working nicely together. It will only take you about five minutes to do, and it could be the most important five minutes of your month.

List what you will do differently over the next month to ensure your priorities better match your life values.

_____

_____

_____

_____

A life-changing experience

At the age of 12, my brother Clinton was diagnosed with a malignant brain tumour that was later classified as a grade four astrocytoma. As far as cancers go, this was one of the worst you could get. Our happy, healthy family now faced a huge challenge: to do whatever it took to make my brother well again. Over the next nine years, my brother went through radiotherapy, chemotherapy and

14 brain operations (including two craniotomies lasting 11 and nine hours respectively). At one point, a doctor told my brother he had six months to live. He suffered from double vision and his eyelids drooped, making it difficult for him to see. Needless to say, it was a difficult time for my brother and our family.

At the time of writing, I am pleased to say that my brother is now 28 years of age and his tumour has been in remission for the past six years. His eyelids have lifted once again and his double vision has lessened. He has completed his university degree, and he even drives a car—something that never seemed possible. Because of his resilience and strength in the face of adversity, he is an inspiration to me and many others.

At one Christmas family gathering, I remember asking Clinton what was the best thing that had happened to him in his life. He looked at me and, without a pause, he said: 'I got cancer'. Now, this might seem like a strange response, but the truth of the matter is that cancer enabled Clinton to start living in accordance with what was most important to him.

On the surface, before he got cancer, Clinton was a picture of success. At the age of 12, he was school captain; he was captain of his cricket team; he was smart, good-looking and great at numerous sports. He was in the top class and was very popular among his classmates.

So, how could cancer make things better?

There was one thing that Clinton realised after getting sick. In his quest to be popular, he had started doing things that he didn't really want to do in his heart. He had started teasing other kids at school, and he had even been caught once by police for underage drinking, at age 12.

Through his illness, Clinton gained clarity about what was most important to him. He was able to gain a spiritual connection with God, and was able to live his life based on intrinsic values rather than the need to be liked. He has learnt to live his life by the values closest to his heart — something from which I think we can all learn. He never once lost faith that he would beat the cancer, even in his darkest hours. He is certainly a living testimony to the power of the mind to overcome extreme adversity. The experience of seeing what my brother went through certainly changed the way I live my life.

Don't wait for a life-changing experience to occur before you start living your life by your values. If your goals don't reflect what is in your heart, you risk not having the life that you deserve.

Chapter 4

POWERTIP: the ultimate goal-achievement system

Life is full of opportunities, but people often don't know how to make the most of them. I have lost track of the number of times I have encountered the following scenario: someone thinks, 'Wow, another brilliant opportunity!' It is the moment they have been waiting for, but there is a problem. They got caught up doing other things and just didn't notice the opportunity until it was too late. 'It's okay', they think, 'there will always be next time ... surely?'

The sad thing is that sometimes there is no 'next time'. Every day, people miss out on amazing opportunities. These missed opportunities can take the form of an article you failed to read; a business associate you failed to ask the right questions of; a potential romantic partner you didn't get around to talking to; the shares you didn't buy; or the university course you didn't know existed. Opportunities are like oases in the desert: they can bring you a new lease on life, but you need to be focusing in the right areas to find them. If you miss an opportunity, you might be lucky to find another one again soon—but there is no guarantee.

Opportunity knocks

It is such a tragedy when opportunity knocks and no-one is listening. It is not as if people intentionally tune out; it is just that the part of the brain that is associated with achievement isn't tuned in to the right frequency. Think for a moment about your favourite radio station: a change in the frequency will make that radio station sound distorted, but when the reception and frequency are spot on, the sound is great. The same applies in life. Your goals, when formed properly, act like a radio frequency that alerts you to brilliant opportunities, with one major difference: you are *always* tuned in, even when you are sleeping! This is because there is a part of your subconscious mind that identifies opportunities and brings them to your conscious awareness. This all happens because you set goals in the right way.

> If not you then who? If not now then when?
>
> —Hillel

Having had the privilege of interviewing a number of top athletes, sporting stars and business executives, I can now recognise the key components of success. All the high-achieving people I've interviewed have one thing in common: they are goal setters. I have yet to meet anyone who is highly successful in his or her field who does not set targets and goals. So, if we recognise that world-class athletes and top business people can attribute their success in part to the fact that they set goals, why do estimates suggest that less than five per cent of people in the developed world set goals? I believe there are a few major reasons for the general failure to set goals, some of which are listed here.

- Some people won't set goals because they don't know what they want. They therefore condition themselves to settle for what they get.

- Many people fear setting the 'wrong' goals. They are so afraid of getting the goal wrong that they never set any goal, and therefore become paralysed by indecision.

- Some people won't set goals because they have 'failed' too many times before. The thought of not achieving new goals makes the process of setting goals too painful.

- A number of people are just not interested in setting goals. They tend to have habits that don't include monitoring and evaluating their achievements.

A friend of mine continually talks about becoming a physiotherapist but, at 32, he has yet to do anything about it. Why? It's that inner voice that says 'perhaps this isn't for me; I would hate to invest valuable time and money into a goal that might not work out'.

On the one hand, my friend is unfulfilled at work; the next 30 years are unlikely to get any easier. A change could be the very thing he needs to inject new life into his career.

On the other hand, he has a family, a mortgage and a stable job, so starting a new career could be risky. However, maybe there is an opportunity that will move him in the right direction. For example, he could do a subject each semester by correspondence (part-time) and therefore gradually complete his studies. That way he could still work full-time, pay the bills and support his family. I believe it would be a real tragedy if he reached the age of 60 and regretted not having attempted the career he was so interested in.

I recently read about a woman, Nola Ochs, who completed her first university degree at the age of 95 at Fort Hay University in Kansas. Why? Because it was something that she had always wanted to do.

 Blake's TIP It's never too late and you are never too old, unless you say so.

American boxing champion George Foreman epitomises the idea that you're never too old to achieve your goals. After a highly successful boxing career that saw him win an Olympic gold medal, the World Heavyweight Championship and many other awards, he retired from boxing to work as a minister. Ten years later, at the age of 36, Foreman decided to return to boxing—and won an amazing 24 straight comeback fights. He was eventually defeated by Evander Holyfield in a world heavyweight title fight at the age of 40, and many said that he had done well, but was now too old to win back the title. Fuelled by a desire to disprove the speculations of the naysayers, Foreman refused to give up. At the age of 45, he defeated 26-year-old Michael Moorer to become the oldest person to win the heavyweight title.

 Blake's TIP Meaningful goals illuminate the path towards your best life.

In 2006, I was lucky enough to be selected as one of the next generation leaders of Australia. Those selected decided that we would, as a group, embark on a program that could make a real difference in Australia. There were two big problems though: it was difficult to get everyone together; and there seemed to be a lot of talk and very little action. I therefore made a conscious decision that, regardless of what happened with this leadership group, I was going to come up with an idea that would make a positive difference in Australia and abroad.

As luck would have it, a few weeks later I was at a video shop looking for a movie to watch when I noticed the movie *Pay it Forward* on the shelf. Starring Kevin Spacey and Helen Hunt, the movie was based on the simple concept that it is important to spontaneously perform acts of kindness for others; instead of recipients paying back the deed to the person who performed it, they were instructed to 'pay it forward', and do a good deed for someone else. I had seen this DVD on the shelf numerous times, but this time was different. This time I stopped and looked at the DVD through the lens of opportunity. I thought, 'Wouldn't it be wonderful to have an international "Pay it Forward Day" to inspire people to perform random acts of kindness and cause a wonderful ripple effect of people making a difference?' Such a day could work as a poignant reminder of the power of giving. The idea came to me only because my goal-achievement brain was switched on.

So what has happened with Pay it Forward Day since the idea's inception? In just three years, the day has spread to 15 countries around the world and has sparked some amazing random acts of kindness. Tens of thousands of Pay it Forward cards have circulated the globe, each one carrying the potential for a total of 24 good deeds (all born from the initial heartfelt gesture). Card recipients keep the card in their wallet or purse until they are ready to pay the random act of kindness, after which they forward the card to someone else in need. Hundreds of schools and businesses have been involved in Pay it Forward Day initiatives, and the day has featured in the media around the world, including four major TV networks, print media and major radio stations.

All this was possible because the initial goal had been etched into my subconscious mind (and, of course, because of a lot of hard work and application by a great team). So what's the vision you have for your life? What would you like to have happen both at work and in your personal life to make it extraordinary?

How to set the right goals for you

While working as a manager at Big White Ski Resort in Canada, I conducted a series of interviews. Candidates were asked where they saw themselves in five years' time. One guy from Vancouver said jokingly that he didn't know where he would be next *week* let alone in a few years' time. I'm sure you might know of others who think in the same way. The question of where people see themselves in a few years stumps many people, and not just in an interview context. How clear is the picture in *your* mind about where you would like to be in five years' time? How about 10 years' time? Imagine you are 10 years older. What would have happened during those years to make you successful in areas of your life? These are important questions, and it really does surprise me how many people fail to give them a second thought.

> The tragedy of life doesn't lie in not reaching your goal. The tragedy lies in having no goal to reach.
>
> —Benjamin Mays

Write a list of everything you'd like to achieve — without limitations

If you've decided that setting goals could have a positive impact on your life, you're ready to take some concrete steps that will assist you to get on the road to success. This first step should be lots of fun!

Write down everything that you would like to achieve over the next few years—without limitations. It is like flipping through a huge catalogue and picking out all the things you want. The key is to write down anything and everything that you would like to be, do or have and evaluate how realistic it may be. Some of you may have grand plans for world domination, while others might just want to enjoy the simple life. It matters not what you write, as long as you write things that represent your personality, values and priorities.

Put on some inspiring music (preferably without words) and take 10 or so minutes now to write down a list of everything you want under the following headings:

□ business and career

□ fun and recreation

□ health and fitness

□ personal growth and development

□ relationships

□ finances

□ spirituality

□ community

□ material possessions.

You might find that you have lots of goals in one or two areas and very few in others, which is fine. Just keep the pen moving and create your ultimate list. Also answer the following questions:

- ☐   What would you do if you knew you couldn't fail?

- ☐   What would disappoint you the most if you didn't accomplish a goal?

- ☐   How would you like to spend a typical weekday?

- ☐   How would you like to spend a typical weekend?

Now that you have completed this task, you should have a large list of things you would love to achieve in your lifetime. Write a date next to each item to indicate when you would like to achieve your goals. The time frames you give yourself might be one, three, five, seven or 10 years.

Blake's TIP   There is power in the moment if there is hope for the future.

You should be feeling a bit excited at this point — many wonderful opportunities lie ahead for you. Now that you have your ultimate list, it is time to pick three to six goals that you would like to achieve in the next year. (When picking goals, remember the core values you wrote down in the previous chapter.)

POWERTIP: formulating your goals correctly

Now that you have chosen some goals that are aligned with your values, and set rough time lines for the achievement of these goals, you need a system that ensures that your goals are properly formulated. The POWERTIP system provides the best chance of achieving success, working equally well in business settings as it does in your personal life.

Each letter in the word POWERTIP is a critical ingredient in the goal-setting process. To increase your chance of success, it is important that you include each ingredient. Even missing just one can have a devastating impact on your results. Figure 4.1 is a snapshot guide to each letter and what it stands for. Each element of the system will be explained in greater depth so you fully understand how it fits in and its relative importance.

Before you write down your POWERTIP goals, I suggest reading the following sections so you have a greater understanding of the importance and relevance of each area.

> So let it be written, so let it be done.
>
> —The Pharaoh Sethi, *The 10 Commandments*

The power of precision

Setting goals that are precise is critical if you are to achieve your goals. For many of us, life can seem like a game of tug of war between competing interests that are vying for our time, energy and attention. To better direct our focus, a precise target is needed. Think of it in terms of electrical power: I could use 100 watts of power in a light bulb to brighten a room. That same amount of power, used in a laser beam, can cut through steel. What's the difference? It is focused, directed power.

Figure 4.1: the POWERTIP goal-achievement solution

P	recise	You should quantify precisely what you want. Knowing exactly what you want will make it far easier to achieve your goal. Vague goals produce vague results.
O	wned by you	Your goal has to be something you have sufficient control over and it needs to be your goal and not someone else's.
W	ritten down	Write your desired outcome in a place where you will look at it daily.
E	lastic	Your goal must stretch you and your capabilities. You must also be flexible enough to change your goal as new circumstances arise.
R	ealistic	Ensure that your goal is realistic. Can you do it? If you can't see yourself achieving it, you probably won't.
T	imely	When will you achieve your goal? Write the date down, and commit to it. Review your goal time frame on a regular basis and update as necessary.
I	nspiring	The goal must inspire you in order to be effective. Why do you want to achieve the goal? There must be a compelling reason.
P	ositively present	Write your goal as if you have it *now* (present tense). It should also be written in a positive way utilising words such as 'achieved' and 'reached' rather than words that indicate loss, avoidance or other negative connotations.

Vague goals produce vague results.

While I was delivering a seminar in Melbourne, an attendee told me that his goal was to be the best real estate sales person in Australia. What a great goal to aspire to! However, this goal was not crystal clear. The wording of the goal was very vague, which might have meant the man's results were less than ideal. Instead of making a general statement about your goal, it's important to be as specific as possible.

If the real estate agent I just referred to had asked himself what being the best really meant to him, he might have been able to articulate his goal more clearly. Did 'being the best' mean achieving the most sales for the year? Or receiving the best feedback from satisfied clients? Perhaps it was about making the most profit? A combination of all three? And the list goes on. Remember, the more precise you can make a goal, the greater the chance you have of hitting the bullseye.

 The sharper the focus, the better the chances of achieving the desired result.

For argument's sake, let's agree that being the best real estate person in Australia means achieving the most profit for the year. If we got that far, we'd be getting more precise, but there is still room for improvement. The question that must be asked in order to really focus the goal is: how much profit is needed in dollar terms? To gain an accurate figure, it is critical to look at the nation-wide sales figures over the past few years to see what the top profit figures were. Is the average profit getting higher each year? What would be a realistic top profit figure for the year ahead? The more precise this number is, the clearer the picture of what needs to be achieved will be.

 Make sure each goal you set is as precise as possible. Say exactly what you want to achieve so it is quantifiable and precise. Herein lies the power of focused attention.

Owning the outcome

When people talk about ownership, they are usually referring to the material possessions they have. For example, I am certain that the TV that I watch, the car that I drive and the bed that I sleep in are *mine*—there is no ambiguity; no question mark; I am 100 per cent certain that I own all of those possessions and therefore can do whatever I want with them. Ownership brings with it a sense of certainty and control. But what has this got to do with goal setting?

Some people set goals that are completely outside of their control. They then get upset or disappointed when they don't achieve what they set out to do. The reality is that there might never have been a chance of success in the first place. The problem is that such goals are flawed from the outset, because the person setting the goal did not own the outcome.

So what does 'owning the outcome' really mean?

Owning the outcome means that you have control over the steps required to reach your goal. In other words, you are not totally reliant on luck or other people to turn your goal into a reality. It means working within your circle of influence. Here are some examples of goals where the person setting the goals does not own or control the outcome.

◻ *My goal is to win the lottery*: Because you have less than one chance in a million of winning the lottery, luck is the key factor that decides whether your goal will be achieved. It is true that 'you have to be in it to win it', but the outcome is still outside your circle of influence.

◻ *My goal is to get my partner to quit smoking*: This is an interesting one. Yes, it is true that you may have a significant influence over the outcome, and you might be able to help your partner quit smoking. However, the decision to stop smoking lies solely with your partner. You can create an environment conducive to change, but ultimately the decision lies with another person. How much does he or she want to change? If his or her commitment does not reflect yours, your goal is flawed from the start.

Make sure that the goals you set are *your* goals and not someone else's. Your spouse, parent or friend might want you to do something, but your level of desire might not match theirs. This will make it difficult for you to maintain any kind of sustained motivation and momentum.

A school friend of mine was expected by his parents to do law at university, and that's exactly what he did. He completed a five-year law degree, but never intended to become a lawyer—his real passion was for writing. Now, I can understand that the law degree would come in handy if he wanted to write books that involved courtrooms or other legal themes, but he'd spent five years living someone else's dream. It's amazing how many people do not begin with their end goal in mind, and therefore do not own the outcome of their goals.

In your organisation, who sets the goals or Key Performance Indicators for employees? Typically, it will be business managers and leaders setting goals—regardless of whether employees like them or not. If the process were more collaborative and less directive, people would be more likely to own the outcome and achieve the goals that they helped set. It helps if employees understand *why* the goals are important, as it provides meaning to the everyday actions required to achieve the goal.

 Blake's TIP When writing a goal, ensure that it is *your* goal and not someone else's. Also, ensure that the goal is within your circle of influence so actualising the goal is more a matter of choice than chance.

The strength of the written word

I often hear people make statements such as, 'I know what I want to achieve—it's all stored in my head'.

That is all well and good ... if it's true! For a goal to be effective, it needs to be stored in your subconscious mind —specifically within your reticular activating system.

In physiological terms, the RAS is a web of cells that spread from your brain stem (medulla) to the cerebral cortex, filtering sensory information to your conscious brain. I like to think of the RAS as the gateway between the conscious and the subconscious mind. In a sense, the RAS determines what you will pay attention to and what you will ignore. At any given second, your brain is being bombarded with approximately two million pieces of information gathered by your five senses. Talk about brain overload! However, it can only process about five to seven pieces of data at a time, so the RAS has the important job of filtering and narrowing the focus.

Imagine for a moment that you are in deep conversation with a friend. You overhear someone nearby mentioning your name. From that moment on, where does your attention go? Are you still listening to your friend, or do you now find yourself wanting to find out what that other person is saying about you? This is a perfect example of your RAS making an executive decision about what to pay attention to and drawing your focus there.

Now that you are familiar with your RAS, you'll understand that it is a very handy tool for being more productive and achieving goals: by setting firm targets in your mind, you are actually reprogramming your brain to prioritise information that relates to your goals. Watch how much quicker your new goals will be achieved with the help of your reticular activating system.

Decathlon Olympic gold medallist Bruce Jenner spoke to a room full of Olympic hopefuls before the 1996 Olympic games. He asked for a show of hands from all those in the room who had set goals. Everyone put their hand up. He then asked who had their goals written down, and who had their goals with them right now. Only one person put his hand up. His name was Dan O'Brien, and he went on to win gold.

This is no fluke. Our mind is incredibly good at manifesting what we want, but we must get the desired outcome embedded into our RAS.

A friend of mine, a fellow director of Life Changing Experiences, set himself two goals when he was at school: the first was to become a millionaire, and the second was to have a brand-new black BMW — both by the age of 18. You can imagine what other people thought: 'As if! How on Earth is that even remotely possible?' But my friend wrote down his goals and then worked extremely hard to reach them. By the time he was 18, he had achieved them.

To ensure writing your goal down has the maximum impact, you should write it down in a place where you will see it every single day. It might be in the front of your diary, on the back of the toilet door, on the fridge, as the screensaver on your computer or on your mobile phone. You could even have it in multiple places to help the goal sink into your subconscious.

> Vision without action is a daydream.
> Action without vision is a nightmare.
>
> —Japanese proverb

In addition to writing your goal and displaying it in prominent places where you're likely to see it on a daily basis, it is a good idea to incorporate imagery into your goal statement. If a picture says a thousand words, then it makes sense to incorporate goal achievement pictures to add power to the written words.

A few years ago, a lady in Brisbane told me a true story about a goal she had set for herself. It was to buy a limited edition Jaguar. She put a picture of the car on the wall of her garage so that every time she would drive into her garage she would be reminded of the car she was going to own—a powerful motivator. Even though others doubted her ability to achieve the goal, she remained highly focused. At the designated time, she had secured the finance she needed to buy her limited edition Jaguar. When she finally reached the dealership, she bought the last one of its kind left in Australia!

 Blake's TIP Display your goals in a prominent place where you will see them daily. Having that constant focus and attention creates energy around your goals. A picture that emotionally engages you on the subject of your goals, placed in a prominent location, will add positive energy to your goal.

Elastic fantastic

The next step in the POWERTIP system is to ensure all your goals are elastic. Now by 'elastic' I am not talking about being able to stretch your legs so you can put them behind your ears (as impressive as that might be). What I mean is that a goal should stretch your current capabilities. It is by stretching that growth and development occur. This is a critical component of goal setting.

It is important not to stretch yourself too far though. Just like a rubber band, if you stretch yourself too much there is a good chance you'll snap. However, most people go the other way—they set goals that they are almost certain of achieving at the outset with minimal effort.

The other component of the word elastic in goal setting is the 'elasticity' of feeling entitled to change your goal if circumstances beyond your control put it out of reach. Rather than scrap the goal altogether or lose motivation, it is okay to shift the goal posts from time to time. Therefore, you may stretch the date out a little bit, or stretch some components of the goal to ensure that it is more realistic. Being able to change a goal as circumstances change can keep you motivated.

It is important not to be *too elastic* once goals are set. Some people might take advantage of the elasticity of the POWERTIP system by shifting the goal posts frequently as a result of personal ineffectiveness rather than outside circumstances. Procrastination, laziness and poor priority management might be the real reasons for which the goal will not be reached on time. It is important to recognise the difference between an excuse and a worthwhile reason that's beyond your control. Telling the truth here is vital, otherwise goals may lose their power—particularly if components are continually being shifted. Some examples of circumstances outside your control are:

- loss of job

- death of a family member or close friend

- global economic downturn

- serious illnesses.

The super-stretch goal

There can be some real value in setting yourself a super-stretch goal—something that would really extend your current capabilities. You might call it your 'big mamma' goal or the 'dream goal'. Sometimes, even if you do not achieve this goal, you will be pretty happy that you got so close. Sometimes we can surprise ourselves in that we can achieve so much more than we ever thought possible. Mark Victor Hansen and Jack Canfield set a goal to sell 1.5 million copies of their book *Chicken Soup for the Soul* by 30 December 1994. Their publisher thought they were dreaming. However, even though they didn't reach that goal, they did manage to sell 1.3 million copies by their goal date—and the books went on to sell more than eight million copies worldwide. Canfield stated that he could live with that kind of failure.

Blake's TIP The sky is not the limit anymore — there are footprints on the moon!

As discussed earlier in the chapter, I set a goal in 2007 to start an international Pay it Forward Day to inspire random acts of kindness around the world—a goal which was definitely a big stretch for me, as I had absolutely no clue how to do it. My stretch goal was to see Pay it Forward Day spread to five countries, to appear on a major national TV network and to build a website where people could share their kindness stories. By just its third year, Pay it Forward Day has appeared on all major TV networks in Australia and one in the US, and the website has received over 800 000 hits. The site has been accessed by more than 50 countries around the world, and some amazing random acts of kindness have happened as a result. Mayors in Salt Lake City, Las Vegas and Henderson have signed their support for the initiative, and hundreds of schools around the world are involved in it.

I think we should all set a super-stretch goal — because you just might surprise yourself and achieve it!

Blake's TIP If things outside your control make your goal too difficult to achieve, shift the goal posts. Also ensure that the goal stretches your current capabilities.

The realm of the realistic

Your own personal beliefs around your goals are important: if you believe that you can achieve your goals, your efforts towards the realisation of your goals will be fuelled. If you subconsciously believe that the goal is completely unrealistic, the chances of achieving it are diminished.

For example, your goal might be to make a million dollars in the next 12 months. Over the past three years your salary has averaged just $60 000 a year. To achieve this goal, the mindset that earned $180 000 over three years would need to be revamped to fully accept the new possibility. If your subconscious mind rejects the new goal and sees it as impossible, this internal barrier is likely to get in the way of success.

When setting your goals, it is important that you feel that they are realistic considering your current circumstances. To own a brand new Audi A3 might be something that you have always wanted, but perhaps it doesn't fit in with the goals the family has of paying off the mortgage in tough economic times.

> If you believe you can, or you believe you can't, you are right.
>
> —Henry Ford

You may have doubt in your mind that you will achieve the desired outcome when setting a goal. That is okay, and is to be expected when you are stretching your current capabilities. But there are ways to shift your mental boundaries to incorporate a new and better way of thinking that is more consistent with your goals. The mental side of goal achievement is something that should not be ignored, and is covered in more depth in chapter 10.

Is your goal realistic?

Sometimes it is hard to be sure that you've set a realistic goal. To get a better idea of how realistic your goal is, I suggest putting it through a testing phase. I recommend replaying the achievement of your goal over in your mind for a few days.

Here's an example of one Jill came up with: 'I am ecstatic now that I weigh 55 kilograms on 3 December 2011'.

Jill currently weighs 85 kilograms and has been on yo-yo diets for many years. The most weight Jill has lost in any one year is five kilograms. She is now aiming to lose 30 kilograms in a year. At first glance this goal might not seem realistic, because the best predictor for the future tends to be the past, and Jill's past results are less than ideal. However, if Jill can shift her mindset and her habits, her beliefs could be positively transformed. By playing her goal over in her mind for a few days, she will start to gain an idea of whether she believes it is possible. If it still feels ridiculous and completely unattainable, then she can change the goal to something more realistic.

Note: health-related goals should always be discussed with a health professional.

 Set goals that you feel you can attain. The stronger your belief that you can achieve a goal, the better your chances of making it to the finish line. You don't need to know how you are going to do it, but having faith in yourself is important. Anything is possible if you put your mind to it!

Timetabling your goals

Time is the most precious commodity any of us has, but still people waste huge amounts of it. I have found that as I get older, time seems to keep speeding up too. It is a shame that so many people do not utilise their time properly to achieve meaningful outcomes.

> The bad news is, time flies.
> The good news is, you are the pilot.
>
> —Michael Althsuler

Each goal you set must have a precise time for completion. It helps harness our efforts: the more precise the time and date of achievement, the greater the clarity.

Blake's TIP Each goal must have a specific time associated with it. Be clear on when exactly you will achieve your goal and commit to it.

Sarah, for example, wants to have $20 000 saved for a deposit on a house by March. This is a good goal, but not a great goal. To improve it, the exact date needs to be worked out. Sarah should instead write: 'It is now 15 March 2011, and I am delighted that I have $20 000 saved for my house deposit'. This goal is excellent because it provides an exact date, and it is written in the present tense (the importance of writing goals in the present tense will be discussed in greater detail later in the chapter).

> A goal is a dream with a deadline.
>
> —Napoleon Hill

In 1990, a comedian from Canada sat in his old Toyota and was upset. He was a struggling actor who was trying to make it in Los Angeles. He took a cheque out of his wallet and wrote the following words: 'Ten million dollars for acting services rendered'. He then dated it 1995. He then kept that cheque in his wallet from that time on. By 1995, he had done three big movies: *Ace Ventura: Pet Detective*, *The Mask*, and *Dumb and Dumber*. Jim Carrey's asking rate for movies at this time was more than $20 million a movie. He had made it. Having a clear date written down gave him the focus and commitment he needed.

> Don't say you don't have enough time. You have exactly the same number of hours per day that were given to Helen Keller, Pasteur, Michelangelo, Mother Teresa, Leonardo Da Vinci, Thomas Jefferson, and Albert Einstein.
>
> —H Jackson Brown, Jr

Inspired outcomes

Meaningful goals energise the spirit to move forward. A goal must inspire you to take action. Quite simply, if it fails to do that, it will be extremely hard to stay motivated and maintain any kind of momentum.

Victor Frankl, one of the few survivors of the oppressive concentration camps of Nazi Germany, worked out that only one in 28 prisoners survived the death camps. As a prisoner in four camps, Frankl was stripped of his clothes, his dignity and every possession he had. His mother, father, wife and brother all died in the camps, and he was exposed to enough death and despair to turn the happiest heart. Frankl was interested in the reason for which some people lived to tell the tale, while so many perished under the horrific conditions. Frankl discovered that the people who survived were not the smartest, fittest or strongest people. Rather, survivors all had a purpose or a goal to aspire to beyond the camps. His love for his wife and desire to see her smiling face again was a major driver.

> The salvation of man is through love and in love. I understood how a man who has nothing left in this world still may know bliss, be it only for a brief moment, in the contemplation of his beloved.
>
> —Victor Frankl

He had control of something that the Nazis could never touch, despite their best efforts: he controlled his mind, and therefore his purposeful attitude (something he called 'logotherapy' in his book *Man's Search for Meaning*). He chose what to think about and what to focus on, and having an inspiring goal helped pull him through the hardships towards freedom.

If I asked you whether it really matters if you achieve your goal, the answer I would expect to hear would be a definitive 'Yes, absolutely'. Make it a 'must' to achieve your goals rather than a 'could, would or should'.

The most popular radio station listened to around the world is WIIFM. It is a frequency that we are naturally tuned in to regardless of age, background, culture, race or creed. It stands for What's In It For Me? At some level in our minds, this question is played out numerous times every day and is a key influencer of the choices we make.

The reasons why a goal is important can help us avoid obstacles and distractions that can get in the way. Let's say you've got just the one tank of fuel to take you to your destination. On the road towards your goal, there are signs for many other attractions that try to get your attention. You might like to go to some of these attractions (or distractions), but by doing so you risk running out of fuel before you reach your destination. Well, that's okay—you can just refuel at a local station can't you? True —but your money is limited and so is your time. If you stop off at too many attractions that require a detour, then you will not reach your destination on time (assuming you make it there at all). These are the challenges we constantly face en route to our goals. Our energy, time and attention can be easily diverted elsewhere and our goals can fall by the wayside as a result.

If the 'why' is big enough, the 'how' will take care of itself. If you have strong enough reasons for doing something, then you will find a way. Where there is a will, there is always a way.

Motivation for achieving goals

Why do you want to achieve your goals? I suggest writing down all the reasons why you must achieve your goals. This will ensure you have a clear and powerful idea of what's in it for you, and whenever your dedication falters, you can always think back to your motivation for achieving your goal.

To better understand your reasoning for setting a particular goal, try to answer the following questions.

- How will it make a positive difference to your life and the people you care about?

- What are the specific benefits that will be gained from its attainment?

- Are you willing to commit the necessary time, money and energy to achieve your goal?

This last question is one that requires some honest reflection. I have known many business executives who wanted a big raise to earn the big dollars, only to find that 'the pound of flesh' they gave to succeed in the role was far more than they were willing to give.

Following are some questions that, if answered thoughtfully, will help you develop a stronger motivation for pursuing your goals.

- How will the goal benefit you?

- How will the goal make a difference to those you care about?

- How will the goal make things easier for you?

- Why must you achieve this outcome by your desired time frame?

What is the one thing that the following people have in common: Martin Luther King Jr; Mother Teresa; Richard Branson; Albert Einstein; Steve Irwin; Lance Armstrong; Christopher Reeve; Helen Keller; Fred Hollows; and Oprah Winfrey?

The answer is they were inspired by meaningful goals. Their motivation helped provide them with the drive and energy to propel them to great heights as historical figures.

For example, many people believe that Christopher Reeve became the real-life Superman after the tragic accident that saw him become a quadriplegic. Upon waking in hospital, Reeve seriously contemplated suicide, as he felt there were no more meaningful goals he could achieve. It was in his darkest hours that he was able to find inner resilience to find a meaningful purpose. He was motivated to walk again one day, and to raise much-needed funds to help others with spinal cord injuries. Even though he never did walk again, he managed to raise $55 million in research grants, and a further $7 million for non profit organisations. His work improved the quality of life of those living with disabilities, as well as raising much-needed funds for medical research. His conviction, determination and positive attitude inspired countless others to see past the pain of the present towards hope for the future.

 Blake's TIP Develop sound reasons for achieving your desired outcomes. The more reasons you have, the greater the motivational reserves you can call on if your commitment falls — you can simply focus on the reasons for achieving your goals to re-ignite your goal-achievement spark.

The power of being present and positive

It is important that your goal be written in the present tense. Research has shown that goals written in the present tense result in a greater acceptance of these goals on a subconscious level. If the goal is written in the future tense (for example, 'I will, at some stage in the future, give up smoking') then you are likely to put off achieving it to a later stage. Not conceptualising their goals in the present tense is a common mistake people make when setting their goals—it really does make a big difference to the likelihood of success.

It is equally important that your goal be written in a positive way. In his book *The Psychology of Winning*, Denis Waitley talks about the drive and power that is created when people strive for a positive outcome rather than trying to avoid a negative one. There is a real difference between 'avoiding the impact of the global financial crisis' and 'making the most out of the global financial challenge'. The difference lies in the wording. Surely someone who has conceptualised their predicament as a 'challenge' rather than a 'crisis' is more likely to feel positive about their ability to succeed. Similarly, 'making the most of' is a far more proactive and empowering way of thinking about the goal than using the negative term 'avoiding'.

Another example of how positive, present-tense wording can make your goal setting as effective as possible might be as follows: *I have now lost 20 kilograms by 30 June 2011.*

The word 'lost' creates a sense of loss in the subconscious mind that can create a negative connotation around the goal. It is better to write the goal using positive language instead, as follows *It is 30 June 2011, and I am so happy now that I have reached my target weight of 70 kilograms.*

The word 'reached' is powerful and positive, and the goal is more precise than the original formulation, because it now has an exact outcome. You will notice that the goal is written in the present tense, so it works well with your powerful subconscious mind.

> **Blake's TIP** Check the wording of each goal you set to ensure it is written in the present tense and that it uses positive words. Your subconscious mind will be more committed towards the outcome you seek.

POWERTIP essentials

If each goal that you set satisfies each component of the POWERTIP system, then you are nicely positioned to achieve what you set out to do.

I suggest you have no more than six (or at a stretch, seven) goals at any one time. The more goals you have, the less energy and focus you can commit to each one. There are a couple of other important factors that are worth considering when setting your goals. Some of these are:

□ If you were to share your goal with key people in your life, would they support you? If the answer is no, would you still be committed to attaining the goal?

□ Does your goal conflict with another goal that you have? If it does, you might consider changing one or both of the goals?

□ Are you committed to doing what it takes to achieve your goal? In other words, are you willing to dedicate your limited time, money and energy towards the fulfilment of your goal?

The great artist Michelangelo said that inside every block of stone or marble dwells a beautiful statue. One must remove some of the excess material in order to reveal the true beauty within. Every one of us has amazing beauty and potential within — it's just that somewhere along the line we lose sight of them. By following the POWERTIP principles outlined in this chapter, you will give yourself the very best chance of success.

> The greater danger for most of us is not that our aim is too high and we miss it, but it is too low and we hit it.
>
> —Michelangelo

Chapter 5

The seven saboteurs of success, and how to blast through them

The world is full of good intentions, but intention doesn't necessarily translate into results. So what goes wrong? Why is it that so many people do not achieve what they set out to?

The truth is that there are some common elements at play that sabotage hopes, dreams and goals. Many of us are so used to these success saboteurs running beneath the surface that we can become chained to outcomes that are far less than we deserve.

Imagine being in a hurdles race. Your goal is to reach the finish line in the best time possible—except there is one problem: the hurdles are invisible. Can you imagine trying to complete a hurdles race where you can't see the hurdles? It would be pretty challenging.

The same principle applies in life. If you can't see the potential obstacles ahead of you, achieving your goals can be very difficult.

It is often said that the best predictor of future results is past performance. I believe that this is a limiting view, because there is considerable power in the moment. Today is a new day with infinite possibilities to do things better than you have in the past. However, in order to improve things, we need to acknowledge and understand what has not worked for us in the past and learn from the experience.

> One who does not learn from history
> is doomed to repeat it.
>
> —Anonymous

Hurdles or obstacles that you have historically faced en route to your goal are likely to resurface in the future if they were not properly addressed in the first instance. This is why it is important that you coordinate a plan to deal with obstacles now rather than leaving your future success to chance.

In order to assist you to recognise potential obstacles, I have compiled a list of the top seven success saboteurs:

1   procrastination

2   excuses

3   pessimism

4   lack of discipline

5   self-doubt

6   fear

7   lack of resilience.

Each of these obstacles will be discussed in detail through-out the rest of the chapter. I will suggest potential strategies that can be used to overcome each one of them.

Procrastination

The fact that procrastination is number one on the list of goal saboteurs should come as no surprise. The word 'procrastination' comes from the Latin word *procrastinare*, which means 'to postpone until tomorrow'. Procrastination steals away valuable goal-getting time, and is a major success saboteur because it kills momentum.

> Procrastination is the thief of time.
>
> —Edward Young

People who are chronic procrastinators often have a case of what I like to refer to as the 'could've, would've, should've' syndrome. Its symptoms include a tendency to say the following things:

'I *could have* done it ...

I *would have* done it ...

I *should have* done it ...

But, I just didn't get around to it ...'

Why don't we get around to our goals? Why do we put them off even though we know it is important for us to achieve them? There are many genuine reasons, but one of the major reasons is habit. The habit of procrastination is one that many people have developed from an early age. If you were someone who left your big school assignment or exam study until the last minute, then you are an experienced procrastinator.

Below are some of the main reasons for which we procrastinate:

◻ We don't want to do the task.

◻ We don't know what to do next, so we do nothing.

◻ We convince ourselves that the task is not urgent and there is no need to complete it right now.

◻ We are fearful of making the wrong decision and therefore make no decision at all.

◻ We are overwhelmed by the size or complexity of a task.

◻ We get sidetracked and lose focus.

◻ We think there are better or more interesting things to do right now.

When I was at high school it was amazing how clean my room would become in the time leading up to my exams. Why? Because cleaning my room was a form of procrastination—I would complete low priority tasks to avoid studying. I remember once cleaning out the big drawer underneath my bed two nights before a major exam.

Somehow, I convinced myself that it needed doing and that now was a good time to do it. That extra hour of study might have helped improve a very average exam mark!

What do you do about procrastination?

To be efficient when it comes to achieving our goals, it's important to formulate the habits of what I call a 'pro-activator'. A proactivator is someone who uses the Nike slogan on a daily basis: 'Just do it'. They know what needs to be done and they stay focused until those tasks are completed.

At this point, I'm sure a lot of readers will be thinking, 'If only it were that easy! Sometimes I even procrastinate after my initial procrastination, only to find myself coming up with another excuse to procrastinate some more'.

There is some good and bad news if you do procras-tinate from time to time. The bad news is that it will take consistent daily effort and focus to change behaviour patterns that lead to procrastination (no, there is no proactivator pill you can take that will magically make you more productive). The good news is that the effort is well worth it, and can have an incredibly positive influence on your life.

The key is to take action. Learn to control your thoughts, feelings and behaviours.

The best and easiest way to break the procrastination habit is by asking yourself these four questions:

1   Am I procrastinating right now? (Chances are that if you are asking yourself this question, you are procrastinating!)

2   Why am I procrastinating?

3   What should I be doing?

4   What will I do to get back on track right away?

Being aware of the fact that you are procrastinating is crucial. This awareness is a skill that can be learnt, and the quicker you realise that you have moved into 'procrastination mode', the quicker you can break the behaviour pattern. Following are some other suggestions to help you move out of procrastination mode and into performance mode.

- If you are procrastinating because the size of the task is overwhelming, break the big task into small, manageable pieces.

- Cross completed tasks off your to-do list. Each little win gives you momentum!

- Reward yourself for completing tasks you don't enjoy. If you don't complete the task, don't reward yourself.

- Create a deadline, or tasks will take far longer than they need to. Tell others of your deadline.

- Focus on how you will feel if you *don't* complete the task by within the time frame you've specified.

- Do the toughest, least enjoyable tasks first.

- Create a distraction-free working environment that's conducive to productivity

- Play some uplifting music to create positive subconscious associations to your work.

And remember, even the most successful people in the world procrastinate. They just do it on their lunch breaks!

Excuses

There are a million and one reasons why we don't achieve what we set out to: commitments; lack of money; lack of resources; lack of skills; the economy; the weather; lack of opportunity; lack of support; insufficient time; lack of clean underwear—and the list goes on. Often it's hard to tell if these reasons are legitimate or if they are just excuses we tell ourselves to make us feel better about underachieving.

In my late teens, I worked on the invention of a swinging tennis ball—one that would move through the air depending on which side of the ball you hit, threw or bowled. It had tremendous retail potential and I saw it as a wonderful opportunity. However, there was a hurdle—how would I patent the invention? I then said something that helped kill the idea: 'It's probably already been patented and I don't really know what to do anyway—at least I gave it a go'.

Five years later, I walked into a sports store and there it was—the swinging tennis/cricket ball known as the 'swing king'. I shook my head and thought back to what had gone wrong all those years before. I had lost an opportunity because I made an excuse and because I failed to persist. I had quit on my goal that day because the going got a little bit tough. It was a powerful lesson that I learnt the hard way.

 Blake's TIP Excuses are the currency of underachievers everywhere.

Take an imaginary walk along an underachiever's foot-path for a minute (although the fact that you are reading this book tells me that you are most likely not on this path). Over a lifetime, an underachiever will find multiple roadblocks that have caused directional shifts, which in turn manoeuvre them away from the goals and opportunities that matter most. There are two different kinds of roadblocks along the underachiever's footpath: one is red in colour and represents real obstacles that are extremely difficult to get past despite your best efforts. These 'red' obstacles might include poor weather causing your flight to be delayed; serious illness; or the passing of a loved one. They can stop you in your goal achievement tracks and sometimes there is very little you can do about it. The second type of roadblocks are orange in colour, and represent mere excuses that block progress. The underachiever actually could get past these barriers with a bit of application, but instead he or she allows the excuse to stop forward-movement.

Let's see how this might play out.

A number of years ago, I worked as a corporate health consultant in Sydney. In this role, I had to offer health advice to over a thousand people. I remember performing a health assessment on a senior executive at a large telco who had a blood pressure reading of 210/130. This was an incredibly high reading, especially considering the fact that the man was already on blood pressure medication! He was also overweight and obviously stressed with work—and with a reading like his, the man was a heart attack waiting to happen!

Apart from alerting him to the seriousness of his situation, I asked him what steps he had taken to get his blood pressure down. Apart from taking his medication, the answer was 'nothing at all'. I then asked him if he exercised. He looked at his watch and replied, 'I'm far too busy and don't have time to exercise. How much longer is this going to take?'

At some level, this senior executive knew he needed to be healthy, but he allowed the excuse of being too busy (the orange road block) to get in the way of improving his health. The truth of the matter was that his excuse of 'no time to exercise' was sabotaging his health. If he had made his health a priority, he would have *found* time to exercise.

Following a seminar I conducted in New Zealand, a woman named Jo approached me about starting her own business. She said she had always wanted to have a successful cake-making business, but couldn't get herself to take the leap. I asked her why. Her reasons were:

▫ 'I have a family to support; it's hard to find the time.'

▫ 'I don't really have the money to start up a business.'

▫ 'I am not too sure how to manage wages, finances and cash flow. I was never too good at maths at school.'

I have had similar conversations with others who have considered making such a leap, and excuses tend to dominate the discussion. It amazes me how often we talk our way out of the very outcomes we seek.

It turned out that Jo worked part-time in a coffee shop while her children were at school and her family needed that money to help pay the bills. She was a very talented cake-maker and her friends and family had always said that 'she made the best cakes'.

So, could she make it work? Could she start a successful cake-making business?

It's a no-brainer, isn't it? It may be difficult and time consuming in the beginning, but where there is a strong enough will, there is always a way. Jo could bake in her spare time and perhaps sell some of her cakes through the coffee house she worked at. She could do a few hours of study each week to learn the financial side of the business, while putting money aside each week to raise capital. She could even contact cake-making businesses in other areas and ask how they got started. Perhaps some of her friends might become her first customers and help spread the word.

It would be such a shame if in five years' time, Jo was still unfulfilled working at the same coffee shop; her dream could become reality with a bit of application, hard work and lateral thinking.

> Ninety-nine per cent of failures come from people who have the habit of making excuses.
>
> —George Washington

I was speaking with a business manager recently about the discipline needed to be a marathon runner. He said that it required commitment to training, sometimes when you just didn't feel like it. At a recent business meeting, he disclosed that he was planning to run the New York Marathon in three weeks' time. A participant piped up saying, 'Well, you must not have any kids to run a marathon!' The business manager responded that he actually had three children. Without skipping a beat, the participant went on to say that he mustn't have a very demanding job then to do all that training. The marathon runner actually held a very demanding, high-powered position within the state government.

This man's line of questioning revealed something quite profound about his own personality: he had a ready-made list of excuses at his disposal and was not afraid to use them. He was likely to miss valuable opportunities due to his habit of making excuses. What he didn't know was that the marathon runner sometimes woke to go running at 5.00 am on Sunday mornings just so he could spend quality time with his family.

I see an excuse as worse than a lie. Neither is very good, but at least with a lie, you are aware that you are being untruthful.

I'm sure you know of someone who has used the following common goal-destroying excuses before:

- 'I'm too busy.'

- 'It's too expensive.'

- 'I'm too old/too young.'

- 'It's not that bad anyway.'

- 'It's too hard to complete.'

- 'I just don't have the resources to make it happen.'

- 'I lack experience and know-how.'

So, what reason(s) do you come up with for not reaching your goals? Are they legitimate ones over which you have little control, or are they excuses you tell to make yourself feel better?

What do you do about excuses?

There are two commonly used words that, when applied to a failure to complete a task, invariably lead to an excuse.

The words are (insert drum roll here): *but* and *because*. For example, the following excuses rely on the words 'but' and 'because':

- ☐ 'I would have gone to the gym, but...'
- ☐ 'I didn't finish the task, because...'
- ☐ 'I was going to apply for the graduate program, but...'
- ☐ 'My sales figures were down, because...'

Of course, after these two words, you can insert any excuse you like. There are legitimate reasons that can follow these two words, but more often than not we justify our less-than-ideal performance with an excuse. That is not to say that a factor beyond your control may not play a part in hindering your performance. However, the key is to know the difference between a legitimate reason and an excuse. Awareness of excuses is the first step to overcoming them. Ask yourself whether your reasons for not completing the task are legitimate, or if they are just excuses.

Awareness is the first step to overcoming excuse-making tendencies. You need to know when you are making an excuse and then shift your thinking towards any positive step you can take towards your goals. The words 'how can I' are critical ones. Rather than say things such as, 'I don't have time', why not say, 'How can I find time?' Similarly, don't say 'I can't afford it'; say instead, 'How can I afford it?' This is a solution-focused approach that empowers you to find solutions and take action.

 Blake's TIP Lose the excuses and breathe new life into your goals today.

Pessimism

Life is a series of decisions that we make on a daily basis. We can choose to be disempowered, upset, frustrated and disheartened by a less-than-ideal result. Alternatively, we can rise above the situation by changing our perspective and focus. Imagine that your mind is a garden for a moment, and that negative thoughts are weeds. How does your garden look? Do you find that you have the occasional weed, or would you be embarrassed to show others the state of your mind garden?

What if JK Rowling had not persisted when the first 12 publishers turned down her first book in the Harry Potter series? The world would have missed out on one of the most-loved book series of all time.

What if Thomas Edison had not persisted after more than 10 000 failed attempts at creating the light bulb? He might not have succeeded in making this world just that little bit brighter (pardon the pun).

What if Lance Armstrong had not bounced back after his life-threatening illness? Millions of people would not have been inspired by his story.

The Beatles were knocked back by several recording companies—can you imagine how the owners of those companies must have felt when they realised their loss!

Choosing to take an empowering meaning from life's disappointments can breathe new life into our goals. For more information about pessimism and its impact on your ability to reach your goals, see chapter 10.

A man found a cocoon of a butterfly. One day a small opening appeared; he sat and watched the butterfly for several hours as it struggled to force its body through that little hole. Then it seemed to stop making any progress. It appeared as if it had gotten as far as it could and it could go no further.

Then the man decided to help the butterfly, so he took a pair of scissors and snipped off the remaining bit of the cocoon. The butterfly then emerged easily. But it had a swollen body and small, shrivelled wings. The man continued to watch the butterfly because he expected that, at any moment, the wings would enlarge and expand to be able to support the body, which would contract in time.

Neither happened! In fact, the butterfly spent the rest of its life crawling around with a swollen body and shrivelled wings. It never was able to fly. What the man in his kindness and haste did not understand was that the restricting cocoon and the struggle were required for the butterfly. To get through the tiny opening was nature's way of forcing fluid from the body of the butterfly into its wings, so that it would be ready for flight once it was free of its cocoon. Sometimes struggles are exactly what we need in our life. If nature allowed us to go through our life without any obstacles, it would cripple us. We would not be as strong as what we could have been. And we could never fly.

— Anonymous

What do you do about pessimism?

When Stephen Waugh was dropped by the Australian cricket team to make way for his brother, he was understandably upset. Instead of dwelling on his disappointment,

Waugh decided to train harder and adapt his playing style to accentuate his strengths. Waugh went on to become arguably Australia's most successful cricket captain, and one of the best players of all time.

 Blake's TIP A positive attitude is the elixir of champions.

So what can you do to avoid being pessimistic? There are three things that can help you overcome pessimistic tendencies:

1   *Awareness*. You need to be aware of when you are being pessimistic so you can alter the pattern. Many people will believe they are positive people, but others who know them well may disagree. It is important that you become aware of when you are doing the following: complaining; blaming; nagging; criticising; annoying; threatening. Perhaps ask others to alert you to when you are doing any of these things so you can increase your awareness. I suggest asking the three people who know you best which one of these habits they think you do the most — this might provide you with some useful insight.

2   *Attitude*. Once you become aware of your pessimism, you can adjust your attitude. Even if you positively adjusted your attitude just five times a day, a big difference to your attitude and goal achievement results over time will ensue. For example, when I worked as a manager in Canada, I asked my team to share the best thing that had happened to them at work in the past week when they came in for

their weekly meeting. This made staff think of all the positive things about their job, which made the meetings much more productive (because they came into the meeting with a more positive mindset).
To adjust your attitude, focus on something good! (Chapter 10 can help you further.)

3   *Action*. There are certain actions that greatly improve your attitude. You may choose to go for a walk; listen to some music; play the piano; or perform some deep breathing. The key is finding what works best for you.

Pessimism is a choice. We all know of someone who lights up a room when they leave it! By having a more positive attitude, we not only brighten up our own lives, but the lives of everyone we come in contact with.

> A pessimist sees the difficulty in every opportunity; an optimist sees the opportunity in every difficulty.
>
> —Sir Winston Churchill

Lack of discipline (the lazy habit)

Lack of discipline is a key success saboteur. The *Oxford Dictionary* defines discipline as, 'the ability to train oneself to do something in a controlled and habitual way'. It involves developing and enhancing good, goal-affirming behaviour habits (something with which many of us struggle). I think we all know of someone, for example, who *intends* to go the gym more often and have a better diet. Somehow, something invariably gets in the way.

My dad is a keen golfer, but his putting is very inconsistent (he would tell you it is consistently bad!). He received a putting machine for Christmas so he could improve his putting, but never seems to find the time to practise. 'Yes, I really should use that machine,' he recently said to me in a frustrated state after missing another straightforward putt. Even if he spent just five minutes a day practising, he would amass over 30 hours of practice over the course of a year. Wouldn't that make a difference?

One only needs to look at Tiger Woods's practice schedule to see why he has been such a successful golfer. His daily practice schedule includes a one-and-a-half-hour gym workout; 18 holes of golf; four and a half hours on the practice tee; one hour putting and another hour working on his short game (close to a 12-hour day!). Tiger's coach believes Tiger deserves his success because of his tremendous commitment and application. After all, talent will only get you so far; not many people are willing to work a 'Tiger day'.

Do you have the discipline and commitment to ensure you stay on track? Alternatively, are you like many people in that you continually get sidetracked into doing other things?

> Discipline weighs ounces while regret weighs tonnes.
>
> —Jim Rohn

Life is a sum of all the choices we make. Each day we must choose between two pains: the pain and effort of maintaining a discipline or the pain of regret (such as Dad wishing he had spent time practising his putting).

To get up one hour earlier to do some exercise is a discipline that some people embrace. To begin with, committing to getting up at such an ungodly hour can be very difficult. The internal chatterbox (your thoughts) will tell you to forget the pain of getting up, and instead get some more sleep. (After all, you are still tired!) Of course, if you *don't* make the time to exercise, then chances are you will suffer the pain of regret for not doing so.

It's the law of compounding return. If you invest small portions of your time, money or energy into something, there will be an exponential, cumulative effect over time. The perfect example is putting money into a high-interest bank account: you begin earning interest on your interest, and your money begins to work for you.

Following are some examples of the decisions we might face regarding the pain of discipline now or the pain of regret later:

- Spend 10 minutes a day keeping a filing system up to date, or face dire consequences later when we spend hours looking for an important document.

- Exercise and eat a healthy, balanced diet, or risk health problems in the future.

- Back up computer files regularly, or risk losing work and wasting our most valuable resource: time.

- Study throughout the year, or to try to do it all in one night before an exam never, realising our true potential.

- Establish and maintain a rapport with all business clients, or risk losing them to someone who will do just that.

❑ Regularly save money to put a deposit on a house or that dream holiday, or risk never being in the financial position to achieve these goals.

❑ Complete extra training to help us get the job we desire, or remain frustrated in a position that leaves us unfulfilled.

Every day you have the decision as to which of the two pains you choose: immediate pain (discipline) versus future pain (regret).

What do you do about lack of discipline?

The key to conquering the problem of lack of discipline is to set up a realistic plan and keep to it. If you have not been good at staying disciplined or committed over a period of time, then the secret is to start small. This way you can gain momentum and increase your efforts as you deem fit. Remember, it's the little disciplines that make a big difference over time.

So, how should you go about improving your lack of discipline?

1 List the small daily disciplines that you could be doing that would help you move closer to your goals.

2 Choose the one or two most effective strategies and commit to putting them into practice in the month ahead.

3 Decide on a review system that works for you. Table 5.1 (overleaf) depicts a simple, practical tool that you could use for reviewing you daily

disciplines each week or month. The idea is to tick off the days that you achieved your intended discipline, and make improvements as necessary. I suggest sticking to the same 10 minutes each week to review your new disciples and your goals.

Table 5.1: daily discipline review tool

This Week's Daily Discipline(s)	M	T	W	T	F	S	S
Eating two pieces of fruit each day	✓	✓	✓	✗	✓	✓	✓
10 minutes of stretching each day	✗	✓	✓	✓	✗	✗	✗
What (if anything) will you do differently next week?							

This Month's Daily Discipline(s) Eating two pieces of fruit	M	T	W	T	F	S	S
Week 1	✓	✓	✓	✗	✓	✓	✓
Week 2	✓	✓	✓	✗	✓	✓	✗
Week 3	✓	✓	✓	✓	✓	✗	✓
Week 4	✓	✓	✓	✓	✓	✓	✗
Week 5	✓	✓					
What (if anything) will you do differently next month?							

Jerry Seinfeld is a great example of someone who enforced the little disciplines he needed for him to become a successful comedian and actor. Jerry decided that the discipline of writing every day was critical to his success, so he put a large calendar up on his wall. On every day that he completed his task of writing jokes, he would put a big red X on the calendar. The idea was not to break the chain of red Xs. This would help Seinfeld to create a positive habit of writing every day. This is a brilliant motivational strategy and certainly worked for him.

Alternatively, you could have an 'accountability buddy' —someone you entrust to hold you accountable to your daily commitments, not accepting excuses that you might come up with. You might even create rewards for yourself for maintaining your discipline and commitment for a period of time (say, for a fortnight or a month).

Self-doubt

Self-doubt kills potential and performance and can form a huge hurdle between you and the achievement of your goals.

The movie *Cool Runnings* has a great scene in it relating to self-doubt. Based on the true story of the first Jamaican bobsled team to compete in the Winter Olympic Games, the scene involves a Swiss competitor suggesting that the Jamaican bobsledder, Junior, go home because he didn't belong there. Following Junior's meek response, Junior's teammate, Yul, dragged him in front of the bathroom mirror. The following dialogue ensued:

Yul: *What do you see?*

Junior: *I see ... Junior.*

Yul:	*You see Junior? Well, let me tell you what I see. I see pride! I see power! I see a bad ass mother who don't take no crap off a nobody!*
Junior:	*You see all that?*
Yul:	*Yes I do. But it's not what I see that counts. It's what you see.*

This final line is the one that stuck with me. Other people are always going to form opinions of you, but the most important opinion is the one you have about yourself.

What do you see when you look in the mirror? Is it a picture of confidence and self-belief or is it one of doubt, fear and uncertainty? Perhaps it is somewhere in between these two extremes, and it might change over time.

In his book *Psycho-Cybernetics*, Dr Maxwell Maltz identifies lack of self-esteem, self-doubt and poor self-image as the main reasons why people fail in life. If everything that went on in your mind was written down and analysed, I think the negative light in which we view ourselves would shock us. We don't have to worry about a backstabbing friend speaking ill of us—we do enough of it ourselves! Following are some examples of how self-doubt can creep into our minds and dominate our thought patterns.

- 'I am such an idiot for making that mistake. I always make mistakes.'

- 'No-one really cares what I think anyway. Why bother?'

- 'There's no way this is going to work.'

- 'I'm not smart enough to be doing this.'

Thoughts you have about yourself have a huge impact on performance. The really sad thing is that many people are aware that they have a negative self-perception, but they continue to let negative internal dialogue occupy their minds. An example of the counterproductive effect of negative self-perception is discussed following.

You have an important meeting coming up and you need to present in front of the bigwigs of the company. As someone who has always had difficulty speaking in front of people, this is a scary thought. There is a lot riding on this talk, particularly as a rumour has been circulating that you might be a candidate for a promotion soon. As you prepare for the speech, your mind starts talking louder to you:

> *You are not a good speaker. Who are you kidding? Get someone else to present for you. It is better than making a fool of yourself. Remember the last time you spoke in front of a big group? Your mind went blank.*

This internal thought virus spreads quickly, making it very difficult for you to do a great job, because you are consumed with self-doubt.

Imagine, instead, if the internal dialogue went a bit more like this:

> *I will do just fine. These people want me to do well and I have prepared thoroughly. I am ready!*

You can see how different this internal dialogue is and how this can make a huge difference in the outcome.

As a keen cricketer, I remember averaging six runs per innings with the bat, which is quite woeful. The following season I completely changed my mental focus: instead of focusing on the thoughts that said, 'I don't want to get a low score', and, 'I'm in bad form', I focused on the great results I was going to achieve. I decided that no matter what bowlers threw at me, it would not be enough to get me out. My average for that season was 133. My ability had not changed, but my mindset had.

One of the greatest powers we possess is the power to choose our thoughts.

What do you do about self-doubt?

So what kind of things can you do to shift the focus away from self-doubt and towards confidence and self-acceptance?

The first thing to do is to stop allowing the destructive, negative voice to dictate proceedings in your mind; letting it talk away unchecked will continue to pull you down and hold you back in life. And the more power it gets, the harder it becomes to perform. Pick an empowering meaning and use more positive thoughts—the results will literally astound you! For more information about how to rewire your mindset to remove self-doubt and increase self-esteem, see chapter 10.

> What you hear in your mind's ear,
> will either give you confidence or fear.
>
> —Laurence G Boldt

Don't let self-doubt hold your potential hostage. Rid yourself of self-doubt and thereby improve your performance. The more you believe in yourself, the more others will believe in you. The more others believe in you, the more you will believe in yourself. And the cycle continues...

> The words you speak, and the words you think, ultimately become the world you live in.
>
> —Robert Kiyosaki

Fear

Fear is a natural part of life, and we all experience it from time to time. Fear isn't always a bad thing. Fear alerts us to dangerous situations that could cause us harm and as such can be incredibly useful. Fear can give us a heightened sense of awareness that makes danger easier to spot and respond to in potentially threatening situations.

Indeed, fear can be a powerful motivator: it can propel us to take action, or leave us paralysed and powerless. Anyone with a phobia knows only too well how fear can paralyse performance. However, fear doesn't need to be of phobic proportions to dismantle our best efforts. It can be a small fear that we just can't seem to get past that stops us in our tracks.

No-one likes to fail or be rejected. In fact, many people would rather not try at all in order to avoid possible disappointment or the pain that comes with it. Fear stops many people from living the life they have imagined.

Figure 5.1 (overleaf) depicts what is known as the fear triangle. It features some of the main fears that we all have, and at the top of the triangle (the apex of fear) is the anticipation of loss. I believe that all fears relate to this one primary fear.

Figure 5.1: the fear triangle

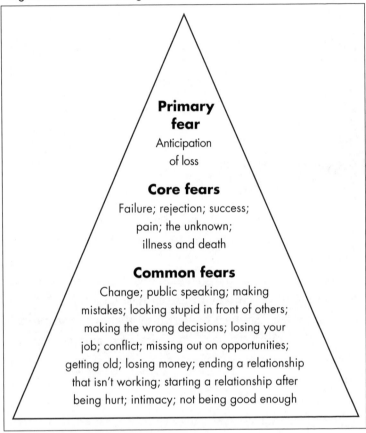

Primary fear
Anticipation of loss

Core fears
Failure; rejection; success; pain; the unknown; illness and death

Common fears
Change; public speaking; making mistakes; looking stupid in front of others; making the wrong decisions; losing your job; conflict; missing out on opportunities; getting old; losing money; ending a relationship that isn't working; starting a relationship after being hurt; intimacy; not being good enough

Specifically, we might fear a loss of the following things:

- dignity
- pride
- self-respect
- friendship
- connection
- sense of belonging

- health and wellbeing
- wealth and possessions
- personal and professional identity
- opportunity.

I certainly can relate to this success saboteur. As a teenager, fear engulfed my every move. Being very shy at school, I found it difficult to talk to any girl whom I liked. I remember the first time that I called a girl on the phone to ask her out. I was completely overcome by nerves, and I had convinced myself that she would never say yes. I had written down exactly what I was going to say — not exactly a picture of confidence! After what seemed like forever, I finally made the call and spoke to her; my heart was beating at a million miles an hour. I asked her out and she said no. Talk about pain. I remember curling up for the afternoon in deep despair. It took me a long time to regain the courage to ask another girl out.

You might not have been such a hopeless romantic as me, but perhaps fear has stopped you in other areas of your life. Have you ever avoided any of the following things because you were crippled by fear?

- asking for a promotion when you felt you deserved one
- starting a course because you doubted your ability to finish it
- speaking to a large group of people when the opportunity presented itself
- telling someone how you really felt
- applying for a job?

> The wall that protects us, also imprisons us.
>
> —Susan Jeffers

How big a role does fear play in your life? Has it stopped you from moving forward? Will you let it stop you in the future?

To confront fear we have to take a certain amount of risk. Risk taking is a double-edged sword. Taking risks can be dangerous, even harmful, as it can dent your confidence, pummel your ego and make you feel terrible. However, not taking risks can leave you frustrated, apathetic and completely miserable.

> To laugh is to risk appearing the fool.
> To weep is to risk appearing sentimental
> To reach out to another is to risk involvement
> To expose feelings is to risk exposing your true self
> To place your ideas before a crowd is to risk their loss
> To live is to risk dying
> To hope is to risk despair
> To try is to risk failure
> But risks must be taken because the greatest hazard in life is to risk nothing
> They may avoid suffering and sorrow, but they cannot learn, feel, grow or live
> Chained by their certitudes, they are a slave, they have forfeited their freedom
> Only a person who risks is free.
>
> —Anonymous

Taking risks is an important part of life, but learning to take positive, calculated risks is a difficult skill to learn. If we risk too much, stress and anxiety can cause major health problems.

I met a high school janitor a couple of years ago who had once been a highly successful entrepreneur. He took some big risks by investing a large proportion of his money into internet stocks and he ended up losing it all—his wealth (millions of dollars), his family (his marriage broke down) and his health (which suffered because of the stress he experienced). He spent two weeks in a psychiatric ward and then spent the next two years housebound. All of this because he risked too much.

With any kind of risk there is always a chance that something unpleasant or unwelcome will occur. So how do you know when the risk is too great? I have found that asking these important questions can help you make an informed decision:

1   What is the worst possible outcome if things go bad? Do you feel you could handle it?

2   Is there a suitable likely return on investment of your time, money or energy?

3   What are your chances of success?

These questions can give you some insight into whether the risk might be worth it. It might be worth getting some feedback from others just to give you another perspective.

If we do not attempt something out of fear, we stay confined to a comfort zone in which there is no growth. It is no coincidence that the most successful people in the world tend to have large comfort zones. Successful people have a higher tolerance for risk-taking, and are therefore comfortable in a broader range of scenarios.

> There was once a very cautious man
> Who never laughed or cried.
> He never risked, he never lost,
> He never won nor tried.
> And when one day he passed away
> His insurance was denied,
> For since he never really lived,
> They claimed he never died.
>
> —Anonymous

Our biggest danger is what happens when we get comfortable for too long. Think of risk-taking as being similar to weights training: the more weights we lift, the stronger we become with less effort. However, the opposite is also true: If we don't step out of our comfort zone every so often, we can become resigned to a limited, repetitive pattern of behaviour. Thus our comfort zone may gradually become our cage, and could eventually cripple us.

It is important to face our fears if those fears are sabotaging our success in some way—and the sooner we can do it, the better.

> Failure lies not in falling down.
> Failure lies in not getting up.
>
> —Traditional Chinese proverb

Figure 5.2 illustrates how the comfort zone can evolve over time.

Figure 5.2: the comfort zone transition

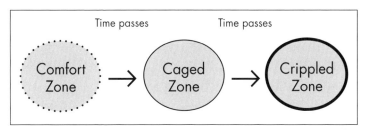

If too much time has been spent avoiding risk, it can become more difficult to break through the wall. This is why the outer edge of the crippled zone is much thicker than that of the comfort zone.

By facing our fears and taking risks, our comfort zone can increase in size enabling us to be more, do more and have more in life. It is outside of our comfort zone that we can learn from our mistakes and grow to our full potential.

What do you do about fear?

I remember receiving some great advice at a Rotary Club leadership course I attended. It was simply this: you only ever fail if you fail to try. This was life-changing for me, as it gave me permission to try things, face my fears and stop worrying about failing. Thinking about it now, there is an even better way of looking at failure — it is a great mantra to live by: 'You are only ever a failure if you fail to try *or* you fail to learn'.

Figure 5.3 depicts the opportunities that lie outside of a comfort zone, including opportunities to learn from mistakes, to gain some new experiences and to grow as a person.

The key message here is that a fear can relegate you to a comfort zone, which can sever your goal achievement chances. By failing to try, you cut off the potential for growth.

By failing to learn (making the same mistake again), your self-esteem takes a battering. By conquering your fears, you empower yourself to move forward, gaining energy that can be transferred into other areas of your life.

Figure 5.3: your comfort zone

Some readers might be saying, 'That's all well and good Blake, but what if I can't get myself to face my fears and move outside my comfort zone?'

Following are some steps that can be taken in order to take control of the fears that may hinder your goal-achievement potential.

1   *Identify the true fear.* To overcome a fear, you must first be aware of what it is you fear most. Often, the *perceived* fear is different from the *actual* fear. For example, speaking in public is a common fear, but the core fear underlying it is usually fear of failure or rejection. It is also worth considering *why* you are fearful (often, fears can be traced back to negative experiences in the past, unrealistic expectations or lack of experience).

2   *Decide to make a change.* Is your fear sabotaging your success in some way? Are you committed to ridding yourself of the fear? The answer to both of these questions needs to be a 'yes' for you to have traction needed to maintain momentum.

3   *Take control of your thoughts.* Assuming you are committed to moving past your fear, you will be able to use the twin forces of pain and pleasure to face the fear head-on. To use these forces successfully, focus on the pain you will suffer if you don't break free from your habit, and focus on how good you will feel when the fear has subsided. Taking control of the thoughts that have led to your fear is a good start.

4   *Be prepared.* Depending on the type of fear you are tackling, preparation can make all the difference. For example, if you fear public speaking, thorough

speech preparation lessens the fear and anxiety attached to giving the speech. You might write down the key points you want to cover and then practise giving the speech to anyone who will listen. If you can't find anyone to practise with, you could draw some smiley faces on some A4 sheets of paper and they can be your practice audience.

5   *Take positive action.* There is no time like the present to remove the 'fear shackles' that hold your potential hostage! Depending on your personality and the fear you are tackling, you might find it better to dip your toes in the water of change or just dive in and overcome your fear head first. Some examples of specific actions that can be taken to overcome specific fears are described in table 5.2.

Table 5.2: suggested actions to overcome some common fears

Fear	Example of a possible effect on lifestyle	Possible actions
Rejection	Not putting yourself out there to meet possible partners	• Perform some daily positive affirmations. • Learn some different approaches and try them on less-than-ideal choices to begin with. This can help bring you confidence to attempt it with more suitable partner types.

Fear	Example of a possible effect on lifestyle	Possible actions
Failure	Avoiding the new computer program at work	• Perhaps you can get hold of a copy of the program and get some assistance in using it at home. Failing that, you could spend some time before or after work learning the program. • Get the thinking right. Think of times that you have learnt things in the past and use positive self-talk, such as 'I can do this'.*
Unknown	Going back to work after bringing up three children	• Talk to friends who have gone back to work after some time. • Get some work experience or complete a course that will help you become prepared for work.

*For more information on how to get your thinking right, see chapter 10.

> Failure is merely the chance to begin
> again more successfully
>
> —Thomas Edison

Step outside your comfort zones, make mistakes, learn and grow. You will begin to unlock your immense potential and achieve your goals.

Note: professional help might be needed to get past some fears (especially phobias and fears that have deep psychological trauma attached), but most fears can be overcome by using the five simple steps mentioned above.

 Mistakes should not be feared — never making mistakes should be.

Lack of resilience

When moving purposefully in the direction of your goals, there are going to be times when things go wrong. Even the most carefully laid plans can go belly up from time to time, and sometimes it can be hard to pick yourself up from the proverbial goal sand trap.

The word 'resilience' comes from the Latin word *resilire*, which means to 'leap back'. It is about responding in a positive way when things go wrong and moving forward despite setbacks.

Can you remember a time when you had your heart set on something and it just didn't work out the way you wanted? You might have done one of the following things:

▫ asked someone out and they said 'no'

▫ missed a crucial goal-scoring opportunity that cost you the game

▫ lost an important sale that you thought was a shoe-in

▫ watched someone else get promoted when you felt you were more deserving

❑   wanted to retire, but the global financial crisis
       adversely affected your retirement fund.

Things don't always go as planned. Life isn't always fair
and you may not deserve poor treatment and lackluster
results. To compound the situation, we often know of
someone that seems to have 'all the luck'. As frustrating as
it seems, it is useful to remember that sometimes good can
come from bad situations.

Let's take basketball superstar Michael Jordan as an
example. Many people might think that Jordan was so
incredibly gifted that he could just waltz into any basketball
team lucky enough to find him. This is not the case. In the
tenth grade, Michael Jordan was rejected from his high
school basketball team. Feeling distraught, he went home
in the afternoon and cried well into the night, such was
the bitter disappointment at not being picked. But what
seemed at the time to be a terrible outcome became a
defining moment for Jordan. He became more determined
than ever before to succeed as a basketball player. From
that day on, Jordan was always the first at training for the
junior varsity team, and worked harder than everyone
else. He went on to succeed on the international stage and
became arguably the greatest basketball player of all time.

The key to Jordan's success was in the way he looked at
his disappointing result: others might have given up and
focused on another sport that they were far less passionate
about, but Jordan focused on what he could do to turn the
situation around. He focused on making the best of a bad
situation, and, as a result, he managed to experience the
career of his dreams.

> If you want the rainbow, you must be
> willing to put up with the rain.
>
> —Dolly Parton

What do you do about lack of resilience?

The ability to bounce back when things go wrong is a critical skill for goal achievers. To gain greater resilience, there are three main areas worth considering.

1   *Change your perception.* Being able to view the adverse situation with a positive lens is a skill in itself. Even though things might be difficult at the time, you can always use self-talk phrases such as, 'This too shall pass'; 'Things will improve'; 'I can learn from this'. The following quote from Zig Ziglar has helped me keep things in perspective: 'You can complain because roses have thorns or you can rejoice because thorns have roses'.

2   *Use positive distractions.* Taking your mind off the situation can sometimes be the best thing for you. You might do this by meditating; having a warm bath; having a holiday; enrolling in a new study course or just reading a good book. Time away can revitalise your energy and help you get your 'mojo' back.

3   *Get adequate support from friends and family.* Having a great support network can lift and inspire you back to your feet in no time. I believe there are five main types of supporters:

1   *Cheerleaders:* friends and colleagues who are always willing to encourage and support you regardless of the outcome. They truly believe in you and your ability.

2   *Challengers:* people who can shift your thinking by challenging your ideas.

3   *Oracles:* people who have great vision and can help you see past your current scenario towards greener pastures.

4   *Trusted advisers:* people who can advise you on the best strategies or steps to pull you out of a difficult situation.

5   *Fun friends:* people who can help you take your mind off the pain. Ideally, fun friends are people you can have fun with and who make you laugh.

I suggest writing down a list of all the people who can offer you support in difficult times. Don't be afraid to call on them as required.

> You don't drown by falling in the water;
> you drown by staying there.
>
> —Edwin Louis Cole

So what do you do when things go wrong?

No matter what difficulties you face, one thing remains true: you have a choice; you can choose what you *think*, and what you *do* on a daily basis, thereby ultimately affecting how you *feel*. No matter what happens, we all get the opportunity to make better choices. We therefore shape our future by the decisions we make each and every day.

There are five steps that can provide a platform that will help you to be resilient in the face of adversity en route towards your goals.

1   *Accept the feeling and the situation.* After all, we cannot change the past. There is nothing wrong with feeling down when things don't go as planned—in fact, I would be more worried if you didn't feel upset!

2   *Analyse the situation.* Was there something you could have done differently to prevent or minimise the impact of the outcome? What have you learnt from the experience? If someone gave you lousy advice, look for a better adviser. If someone let you down, seek a better alternative. If you made a mistake, learn from it and move on.

3   *Modify your goal.* Based on the situation, decide whether you need to change your goal. If a situation has put your goal out of reach, maybe it is time to work out a more realistic goal.

4   *Surround yourself with people who can support you.* A problem shared is a problem halved.

5   *Persist.* Tomorrow will be a new day, and no matter what happens, the sun will still rise in the morning (even if it is behind some clouds).

The obstacle override technique

Power generators are a great back-up system when things go wrong. Floods, lightning strikes and hurricanes are just some of the disasters that can cause power outages with devastating effects. Without power, food in fridges goes off; heaters are useless in cold climates; and of course, TVs won't run! On a more serious note, power failures can create a life-or-death situation if you have a medical condition that requires certain equipment. Back-up generators or emergency power systems can keep things running smoothly.

Similarly, from a goal-achievement perspective, things sometimes go wrong. People and events can take the wind from our sails if we don't have a back-up plan ready to maintain energy and momentum. Ideally, we don't want these negative experiences to kill off our goals. This is where the obstacle override technique can help.

This technique takes only a few minutes to complete, and provides a useful snapshot of the best ways to break through the obstacle that stands between you and your goal. The obstacle override technique is explained following.

Step 1: identify the biggest barrier to success.

Step 2: answer the question: is it within your circle of influence to do something about it? If the answer is no, who can help?

Step 3: assuming the answer to the previous question was yes, the next step involves listing all possible actions that you could take to get around, over or through the barrier. Talking to others can give some great perspectives that you may not have thought of.

Step 4: rate each approach based on the following factors: ease of implementation; likely effectiveness; and return on investment of time, money and energy. Do you believe your chosen approach will work?

Step 5: decide on the best approach to take, and set a time frame if appropriate.

Step 6: take action and execute your plans.

Step 7: review your progress and make adjustments as necessary.

It's hard to win a hurdles race when you can't see the hurdles. Knowing the obstacles that could block your goal-achievement path is one thing; taking action to avoid or blast through the obstacles is another.

Many said that Mount Everest was too tall and could not be climbed. Along came a New Zealand man who proved that anything is possible. He had this to say about conquering the world's tallest mountain:

> It is not the mountain we conquer, but ourselves.
>
> —Sir Edmund Hillary

Chapter 6

Habit shift: removing limiting habits

As the old saying goes, 'Old habits die hard'. Feeling as if you're chained to bad habits can be very frustrating. It's even worse when those same bad habits get in the way of the achievement of your goals and dreams. That's why we all need a reliable system that gets rid of bad habits once and for all. This chapter will explain how habits become entrenched and what you can do to break them.

What is a habit?

I define a habit as an action performed so regularly and repeatedly that it becomes ingrained at a subconscious level. In other words, the brain has more or less developed a shortcut for performing the task, which means that minimal thought and focus are required to complete it.

> We are what we repeatedly do.
> Excellence, then, is not an act but a habit.
>
> —Aristotle

Although it is impossible to speculate about the exact number of habits people have, I would suggest that most of us would have thousands. The way we talk, walk, dress, think, dance, sing, drive, work, drink, eat, sleep and so on are all habits. It is true we have some habits that we would rather forget, but there are some other habits that are very good. For example, I am unable to get to sleep at night unless I have brushed my teeth. This is because the habit is so well entrenched in my subconscious psyche.

How do we develop habits?

Habits start at the conscious level, and begin with a process that I refer to as *pre-habit*. A pre-habit is the initial stage of habit development where although an action is repeated many times, the mind must consciously think through each step of an activity required to achieve an outcome.

The perfect example of a pre-habit is a toddler taking his or her first steps. You can see the level of concentration required for the child to coordinate his or her movements and balance in order to walk. Eventually, walking becomes a habit that doesn't require a second thought.

Likewise, when people learn to drive a car, they go through an important pre-habit phase where the feet, hands and senses learn to work together to move the car in a controlled fashion. With practice and repetition, a habit is born and the behavioural pattern required for effective driving becomes automatic. Experienced drivers can drive without having consciously thought about the driving process at all. So you can appreciate that habits are useful, because they free up our minds to focus on other (more important or more interesting) things.

Just as good habits can be beneficial, bad habits can be equally detrimental because they are ingrained at a subconscious level, and therefore harder to unlearn. That's why people often find it difficult to discard a habit they know is bad for them. When fruit goes off, you don't leave it in the fridge for months on end to fester, do you? When you realise that the fruit is bad, you get rid of it. So why don't we get rid of the bad habits that hang around like rotten fruit? There is a multitude of reasons, including:

▫   lack of awareness

▫   lack of know-how

▫   lack of commitment.

People with bad habits will often say things such as, 'I can't believe I keep doing it. I know I shouldn't, but I just can't seem to stop'.

Smoking is a great example of this.

The research on the negative impacts of smoking is readily available and iron clad: smoking considerably increases your chances of developing all kinds of health problems, including cancer and heart disease. In fact, tobacco use kills between a third to a half of people who use it. The World Health Organization (WHO) released a report in 2008 with some damning statistics on smoking. Among other things, the report concluded that: 'Tobacco is the only legally available consumer product which kills people when it is used entirely as intended'.

Here is the really interesting part: assuming that most smokers are aware of the negative health effects of smoking (which is certainly the case in developed nations), why do more than a billion people around the world smoke? Why, with each generation, do people continue to take up this habit? And why do so many people (regardless of their age) find it so hard to quit? Clearly, just knowing that a habit is bad for you is not enough to break the habit. There must be other factors at play.

So, why don't people break habits that they know are bad for them? The simple reason is that it is easier not to change; it takes less effort to continue practising a bad habit than it does to reinforce a new one.

A loaded gun is a dangerous weapon, but it remains harmless until the trigger is pressed. Similarly, bad habits tend to fire when an emotional trigger is present. Each bad habit that we partake in has a trigger. For example, assume that overeating is a bad habit that needs to be shifted. One person's desire to overeat may be triggered whenever he or she feels too much stress, while another's bad habit may be triggered by boredom. Each individual needs to learn what his or her triggers are, and find effective ways to avoid or deal with them.

Each of us will have our own unique trigger, so there is real power in knowing the emotional precursor to any unwanted behaviour. By knowing the trigger, you can either avoid situations where the trigger is likely to occur, or choose a more empowered response that satisfies your emotional need. If a bad habit is triggered enough times it can become entrenched, making it more and more difficult to break.

What is entrenchment?

Some habits are quite easy to break free from, while others grab hold of you and cling on despite your best efforts to shake them off. These are what I call 'deeply entrenched' habits. Just as negative beliefs can infect our minds, entrenched habits are like the bouncer in the nightclub of change: no matter how hard you try to go through the 'change door', the bouncer tends to stay firm.

These entrenched habits occur when you have established a habit so firmly that change is very difficult or unlikely. So when I talk about levels of entrenchment, I refer to how deeply ingrained a habit is within your subconscious mind. The longer you have been reinforcing a habit, the harder it is to break away.

In figure 6.1 (overleaf), at the lowest entrenchment level are pre-habits. At this level of entrenchment, habits have the potential to turn into full habits, but a great deal of conscious thought goes into the action or activity. As you move further to the right of the scale, your subconscious mind begins to take over from the conscious mind; you start finding that when performing the activity involved in the habit, you no longer need to think about what you are doing on a conscious level, because it becomes automatic. At the 'extremely high' end of the scale, you may feel trapped into a certain behaviour pattern. It often requires significant effort and/or strong reasons to break free of the habit.

Figure 6.1: the habit entrenchment scale

Very low	Low	Moderate	High	Extremely high

The habit entrenchment model

I devised the habit entrenchment model to help you to plot your habits graphically on a grid (see figure 6.2). This way you can easily see where your habits and entrenchment levels are at any one time. On the horizontal axis, you have the habit rating scale, which classifies habits on a scale that ranges from extremely beneficial to extremely destructive. On the vertical scale is the entrenchment level, which signals how ingrained and strong a habit is. The level of entrenchment is particularly affected by time (years of repeating the habit) and the depth of emotional response to the habit (the higher the pleasure or pain response, the greater the potential entrenchment).

As can be seen by the model in figure 6.2, each quadrant is represented by an animal.

Figure 6.2: the habit entrenchment model

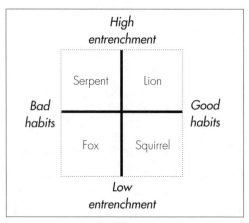

The serpent quadrant characterises a bad habit that has high entrenchment attached to it. The serpent habit has the potential to be poisonous to the spirit, and includes extreme habits known as phobias and addictions.

Examples of habits that might fall in the serpent quadrant include:

▫ problem gambling

▫ chronic poor organisation

▫ smoking a pack of cigarettes a day

▫ frequent negativity.

Any bad habit can make its way into the serpent quadrant if the behaviour is repeated enough times to create higher levels of entrenchment. It is possible to break through these bad habits, but it takes plenty of commitment, support and sometimes professional help.

The fox quadrant represents sneaky, underhanded bad habits. 'Fox habits' can creep up on you and, before you know it, they have managed to infiltrate your mind and moved into the serpent quadrant. The fox quadrant contains bad habits that have not yet become fully entrenched in your subconscious mind, but certainly have the potential to move in that direction.

> Chains of habit are too light to be felt until they are too heavy to be broken.
>
> —Warren Buffett

Habits that might fall into the fox quadrant include the following:

◻ social smoking

◻ occasional procrastination

◻ eating junk food a few times a week

◻ infrequent complaining.

It is much easier to rid yourself of a negative habit in the fox quadrant than it is to rid yourself of a habit that has reached serpent status.

The bottom right area is the squirrel quadrant. The squirrel represents the habits of an individual who is hardworking but easily distracted by what's happening around him or her. The habits in this quadrant are good, but the level of entrenchment is only low to moderate. This means that the habits in this quadrant have only recently formed, and might still be in the pre-habit phase.

Habits that might fall in the squirrel quadrant include the following:

◻ drinking two litres of water on most days

◻ reviewing goals on a semi-regular basis

◻ keeping promises most of the time.

The seeds of good habits are born in this quadrant, and with the right amount of watering they can blossom into entrenched habits. With repetition and reinforcement, these habits can move into the most desirable quadrant: the lion quadrant.

The lion quadrant is the king of the habit quadrants: it signifies pride in one's beneficial habits, which are now firmly entrenched into the subconscious mind. Real strength can accumulate in the powerful habits that positively shape your character. Habits that might fall in the lion quadrant include:

- utilising an effective organisation system daily

- always telling the truth

- exercising regularly

- being proactive.

The lion quadrant brings out the best in you, often inspiring others do the same.

When you place your habits into this model, you would most likely find that you have habits in each quadrant. Highly successful people tend to have a lot of habits in the lion quadrant; they don't have to think much about what they need to do in order to achieve their goals—they just do.

What habit do you want to change?

The first step to any kind of change is awareness: you need to know which habit you would most like to shed, and have a strategy to change it. The following is a list of good, bad and ugly habits that you may possess—both relating to your work and your personal life. Following is a breakdown of the difference between the three types of habit.

- Good habits benefit you both in the short and long term.

- Bad habits can hinder your performance in many different life areas.

❑ Ugly habits can cause major problems for you in the future if they are not dealt with.

See if any of the good, bad and ugly habits discussed following apply to you.

Personal habits

Everyone has one or two bad habits that affect their personal life. Table 6.1 outlines some common good, bad and ugly habits.

Table 6.1: good, bad and ugly personal habits

Good	Bad	Ugly
You maintain good posture.	You slouch too much.	You are fast becoming the hunchback of Notre Dame.
You are very punctual.	Occasionally you are late.	You tend to be embarrassingly late all the time.
You exercise four or more times a week.	You rarely exercise.	The most exercise you do is turning on the TV.
You eat a balanced diet with plenty of fruit and vegetables.	You constantly consume large amounts of fat, sugar and salt.	Your best friends are Ronald McDonald and Mr Whippy.
You take good care of your lungs.	You smoke socially.	You smoke a couple of packets of cigarettes a day.

Good	Bad	Ugly
You take responsibility for your actions.	Occasionally you make excuses and blame others when things go wrong.	You have the classic victim mentality: nothing is ever your fault, and you remain resistant to any kind of personal change.

Work habits

In the workplace, certain habits can affect our ability to do a good job and engage well with our colleagues. Some common good, bad and ugly habits are described in table 6.2.

Table 6.2: good, bad and ugly work habits

Good	Bad	Ugly
Work colleagues can depend on you.	You are seen as unreliable in your workplace.	You constantly let people down.
You promote harmony in the workplace: people like working with you.	You continually complain about your job.	You undermine the bosses' authority and spread negative rumours.
You always do what you say you will do: you have high levels of integrity.	Occasionally you make promises you can't keep.	People at work are calling you Pinocchio behind your back.

Table 6.2 *(cont'd)*: good, bad and ugly work habits

Good	Bad	Ugly
You always keep files up to date.	You let filing build up for another day.	You have no workable filing system.
You always treat the customer as number one priority.	You are not really that concerned about your customers.	You treat the customer with disdain.

The habit you would most like to change may or may not be on this list. Ask a family member, friend or co-worker what he or she believes is your worst habit. Sometimes we can be surprised by bad habits that we don't even know we have!

To help you identify the best habit(s) to change, I have put together a system to assist you to build strong psychological and emotional foundations for the task of breaking bad habits—permanently.

Bad habits are like a comfortable bed.
Easy to get into, hard to get out of.

—Anonymous

The four pillars of habit shift

The Burj Dubai tower is the largest man-made tower in the world with a height of 818 metres encompassing a total of 160 floors. To understand just how tall it really is, remember that New York's Empire State Building is just 450 metres tall—just over *half* the height of the Burj Dubai. To withstand extreme weather conditions including gale force winds and storms, the building needs a strong foundation; over 45 000 cubic metres of concrete (weighing more than 110 000 tonnes) was used to construct the foundation and the structure itself included 601 metres of vertical concrete pumping—a world record!

Just as the Burj Dubai needs strong foundations and support, we human beings need solid foundations when build-ing better habits. The four pillars of habit shift explained in this chapter provide you with the support you need to overcome bad habits, and will help you to build a better structure that will enable you to maintain the change you are committed to.

After delivering a speech in Brisbane, I met a woman called Kelly. She was a heavy smoker who had lost her husband to lung cancer when he was 54 years old. Her father had died of smoking-induced emphysema. Kelly asked me why she couldn't quit smoking when she really wanted to. Indeed, she had two strong emotional reasons to give up (not including the obvious threat to her own health), but she continued smoking a pack of cigarettes a day. So, why did she continue to smoke?

Kelly certainly had great reasons to quit the habit, but there was an important reason why she couldn't: she experienced strong 'payoffs' or positive effects while smoking, and these payoffs overshadowed the negatives of her habit. Indeed, with *every* bad habit, there are reasons or benefits for continuing to engage in the practice; otherwise, you just wouldn't do it.

So what were Kelly's perceived payoffs for continuing to smoke? Stress relief and time out with work colleagues (cigarette breaks) were the main perceived benefits of smoking, and over time the association between smoking and these payoffs became very strong, resulting in her habit becoming deeply ingrained. There was also the physical addiction involved, which made smoking difficult to give up.

Table 6.3 demonstrates some of the perceived payoffs that go hand-in-hand with poor habits.

Table 6.3: poor habits and their perceived payoffs

Bad habit	Perceived payoffs
Laziness	• More relaxation time • Lower expectations from others • Less pressure to perform
Eating junk food	• Pleasant taste • Requires little effort • Inexpensive • Saves time
Procrastination	• More enjoyable tasks are completed first • Requires less effort than work
Lying	• Avoidance of painful truths • An appealing illusion of reality is created

To break free of bad habits, we need a system that can move us away from the payoffs. The four pillars of habit shift that are discussed following are a great system to help you do this.

The first pillar: reason(s) to change

The first pillar of habit shift is finding strong reasons to change — reasons that are stronger than the perceived payoff. If there is not strong enough reason to change, let's face it: most people won't. I believe in Kelly the smoker's case, there were very compelling reasons for her to change — a great start!

It is important to be crystal clear about why you need to break the pattern. Keep in mind that the better your reasoning, the greater your conviction will be that breaking the habit is the right decision. So write a list of each reason (big or small) to give yourself the leverage you need. Then, read this list on a daily basis. By repeating the reasons to change, your mind will find it harder to access the payoffs.

A recent study was conducted by a group called The Fun Theory at Odenplan subway station in Stockholm to see if they could get more people to take the stairs instead of the elevator. They turned the stairs into musical notes (like a piano) and what they found was 66 per cent more people used the stairs instead of the elevator. Why? Because there was now more of a reason to use the stairs (because now it was fun).

The second pillar: belief

The second pillar of habit shift is often overlooked: it is the belief that you can change. Without the right mindset it is extremely difficult to make any lasting, positive changes. I have met a number of people who say that they believe in their ability to make a change, but they lack any real conviction. You only need to examine someone who has been on the rollercoaster of losing weight and then gaining it back for many years to be able to spot someone who has no real belief that they can change. They often develop a belief that they can't maintain their target weight, and this belief undermines so much of the positive work they might do. If your mind does not support the change you wish to make, then it is like walking up an escalator which is going down—it can be hard going! Controlling the internal dialogue in your mind to speak positively about the change you are creating is a good start. Creating the right belief and mindset is examined further in chapter 10.

The third pillar: focus

The third pillar of habit shift is focus. This pillar turned out to be a critical one for Kelly, the woman who couldn't quit smoking. Kelly had strong reasons to change, and a belief that she could change. However, her inability to focus on the reasons for quitting led her to disregard their importance; instead, she focused on the perceived payoffs of smoking, which resulted in her continuing to smoke.

Let me explain: when Kelly was not smoking, she could talk about quitting, and she clearly believed that she should make the change. In these moments, there was no emotional attachment. However, whenever she felt stressed she would focus entirely on the enjoyment that she would get from smoking (the payoff). At the critical 'trigger' moment, Kelly would focus on the perceived payoffs rather than the reasons to change the habit. Imagine how much stronger Kelly's drive to quit smoking would be if she had a picture of her father and husband on each side of the cigarette pack; imagine if she focused on what smoking did to them when she was considering lighting up another cigarette. Smoking would most certainly cease to be a pleasurable experience for Kelly if she focused on the reasons she must change rather than the payoff involved in the critical habit trigger stage.

So how do you get your focus right? When you find yourself thinking about indulging in the bad habit, draw your focus away from the payoff and onto the reasons you need to change. Once you have done this, the fourth pillar, action, is needed for effective habit shifting.

The fourth pillar: action

The fourth and final pillar of habit shift is the action pillar. This refers to the implementation of practical steps to become free of the habit you are trying to change. It is a critical step that often gets overlooked.

So what actions am I talking about? It will obviously depend on the habit involved. The key is to find appropriate actions to replace the bad habits. In a sense you need to discover a better routine. For example, if you have a habit of being disorganised, it will take some time and effort to shift it. You might adopt the 'use it, file it or lose it' paper management system on a daily basis and have periodic reminders as a way of reinforcing the habit. I would suggest putting a gold star or tick in your diary for each day you perform the good habit. This can act as a great visual motivator for you to keep the positive change going for at least a month. Table 6.4 depicts some actions that can act as a conduit towards positive habit change.

Table 6.4: positive habit change action steps

Bad habit	Possible action steps
Procrastination	• Break down the project into smaller, more manageable tasks. • Do the most difficult tasks first and create some meaningful rewards for achieving key milestones. • Think about the project in a different, more positive way.
Gambling	• Find healthier ways to achieve excitement and variety (as these are the likely needs not being met). Ideas include fishing, scuba diving, canyoning and reading.
Eating too much	• Drink a full glass of water every time you feel like over-eating (many of us confuse thirst for hunger). • Make a conscious effort to eat your meals more slowly. • Never shop when you are hungry. • Have healthy, low-fat snacks on hand.

Finding the right actions to manoeuvre you away from your bad habits is essential. As for Kelly, she needed new ways to deal with stress. For her to break free from the habit, two out of the four pillars needed adjusting—namely, focus and action. Specifically, Kelly decided to chew gum when she was feeling stressed, and to have regular power walk breaks, where she listened to funny podcasts on her iPod.

So the big question is, did Kelly quit smoking? Yes she did. She even emailed me a while back saying she was going to compete in a sprint series triathlon.

Relapse

It would be remiss of me to fail to include a discussion of relapsing into old habits.

Relapse is extremely common; in fact, the profitability of the entire diet industry (worth between $40 billion and $100 billion US) depends on people relapsing into their old eating habits!

But surely, you might think, after you've shifted a habit, you've stopped for good: the neural pathway created by the old habit is removed over time ... isn't it?

Research shows that this is not the case. MIT professor Ann Graybiel argues that 'Important neural activity patterns in a specific region of the brain change when habits are formed, change again when habits are broken, but quickly re-emerge when something rekindles an extinguished habit ... It is as though somehow, the brain retains a memory of the habit context, and this pattern can be triggered if the right habit cues come back'.

Therefore even if you have given up a habit for some time, or if you are in the quitting phase, the habit could return. The important thing to do is to try and avoid the old triggers and if there is a relapse, learn from it, and commit to the change you made in the first place.

The seven habit shift essentials

People whose habits have moved into the serpent quadrant need a powerful approach to shift their habits. The seven habit shift essentials detailed following will enable you to shed a bad habit for good.

1   You must be open to change. Challenging certain behaviours and telling the truth about what is not working enables you to break free of habits that weigh you down.

2   Know your triggers (the occasions when temptation can cause a habit relapse) and arm yourself with strategies to deal with them. Consider avoiding situations or people who may tempt or distract you from achieving your goal of breaking the habit.

3   Plan your approach using the four pillars of habit shift. To do this, complete the following steps:

    1   Develop strong reasons for changing.

    2   Believe you can change by feeding your mind positive thoughts.

    3   Shift your focus away from payoffs to the reasons to change at the trigger moment(s).

    4   Take positive action to install a better habit each day; discover what works best for you.

4   Devote your energy and attention to changing only *one* bad habit each month.

5   Stay on track: if you slip up, don't give up! Don't beat yourself up about it; we all make mistakes from time to time. Instead, learn from the experience. Perhaps you need a new focus point or action to help you continue in the right direction.

6   Tell others who can support you about your plans to break your habit, and ideally enlist the help of someone who holds you accountable.

7   Celebrate each day you manage to avoid the bad habit and reinforce the new one. You might consider putting a gold star on a calendar or chart for each successful habit-breaking day. Reward yourself at the end of the month if you achieve what you set out to.

Over the past years, I have been lucky to work with some amazing people and have seen some amazing changes Imagine if you committed to having 12 better habits (one each month) in the year ahead. Wouldn't that make a big difference to your chances of achieving your goals? If you follow the seven steps, there is no reason that you cannot achieve everything you set out to this year and beyond.

Chapter 7

Implanting goals into your subconscious

A clear, vivid picture in your mind can be a powerful motivational force that can drastically increase your goal-getting potential. Indeed, many of the world's most recognised athletes, actors, artists and pioneers have used the techniques that I will discuss in this chapter to propel them to greatness. Arnold Schwarzenegger used visualisation techniques to help him become Mr Universe. Michael Phelps visualised winning a record eight gold medals at an Olympic game many times before he actually achieved it. When Sir Edmund Hillary became the first man to reach the peak of Mount Everest, he was asked what the feeling was like. Hillary replied that it felt exactly the same as the previous times he had done it—in his mind. This chapter will explain how visualisation works, and how you can harness its considerable power to achieve your goals.

What is visualisation?

Visualisation involves rehearsing various scenes of success and achievement in the fail-safe surroundings of your mind. This internal safe environment acts like a 'dress rehearsal', where you can address any stumbling blocks (such as stage fright or performance anxiety) in order to face and conquer them in reality.

By using powerful visualisation techniques, it is possible to imprint goals deep into your subconscious mind. This is important for goal achievement, because everyone naturally gravitates towards the goals that are etched into their subconscious minds. When you have your goals imprinted on your subconscious, you become like a homing pigeon or a target missile: you create an almost magnetic force between you and your goal.

To explain what I mean by visualisation, I'd like you to try the following quick exercise.

Imagine yourself taking a fresh orange from the fridge. Hold it up to your nose and draw in that lovely fresh orange scent; enjoy the brightness of its colour, and feel the cool, dimply exterior. Walk over to the chopping board and slice the orange in half and then again into quarters. Now raise a quarter up to your nose and breathe in the smell of freshly chopped orange. Feel its juices run over your fingers. Now, with the smell of this fruit still clear in your mind, raise it up to your lips and bite into it. Enjoy!

So could you picture it? And is your mouth watering? If a simple little exercise like this can evoke an involuntary reaction such as salivating, just imagine what embedding a vision into your subconscious can do for creating an internal drive towards achieving your goals! Norman Doidge, MD—author of the best-selling book *The Brain That Changes Itself*—argues that 'in action and imagination many of the same parts of the brain are activated'. This explains why your mouth watered when you imagined biting into the orange. This is great news for goal achievement. The deeper you embed goal achievement images in your subconscious, the greater your likelihood of success.

Why is visualisation so important?

Natan Sharansky, Soviet human rights activist and chess champion, used visualisation to stay alive. He was imprisoned for treason by Russian authorities for nine years, 400 days of which he spent in solitary confinement in a dark five by six foot hole in freezing temperatures. When others would lose their minds for lack of external stimulus and contact, Sharansky managed to pull through with the use of visualisation. Although it sounds quite strange, he actually played chess in his mind to get himself through the toughest of those times. After his release years later, Sharansky had the opportunity to play against the world chess champion, Garry Kasparov. He performed so well that the world champion could not defeat him!

I know of one lady, Maxine, who was a badly addicted smoker. With a loving husband and two sons, she was aware she needed to stop smoking—both for herself and for them. She tried several times to quit, but always regressed. Finally, Maxine tried a method known as pain visualisation. This involved reading up on the negative health consequences of smoking and visualising these symptoms as if they were actually happening to her. She would wake in the middle of the night in a sweat and be convinced that she had lung cancer—to the point where she could hardly breathe. She stopped smoking as a result of the visualisation technique, and has not smoked a cigarette for 15 years.

When my brother Clinton was fighting for his life, I created a visualisation CD for him to listen to daily. It had music, sound effects and character voices on it, and its aim was to give him a mental picture of the brain tumour being destroyed. Fourteen years later, Clinton is cancer free after being given just six months to live at the age of 16. Although there were a number of factors that contributed to Clinton's recovery, I believe that picturing a favourable outcome can help create a positive mental environment that is conducive to healing.

Throughout history, some of the most successful artists, sportspeople and entrepreneurs of all time have described visualising their goals to focus their actions and help them maintain the necessary motivation for goal achievement. The great artist Michelangelo, for example, would see the sculpture clearly in his mind before he started chipping away at marble or stone; Walt Disney had a vision for Disneyland long before a single ride was constructed.

For hundreds of years, athletes have used visualisation techniques to help them achieve peak performance. For example, a professional soccer player will often rehearse the perfect outcome of a penalty kick over and over in his mind before actually doing it under the pressure of competition. The neurological basis for the success of this technique was demonstrated by soccer star David Beckham, who once participated in an experiment where his brain waves were measured as he took some free kicks at goal. He was then asked to *imagine* himself taking free kicks while sitting in a comfortable chair. The brain patterns that showed up on the computer screen were nearly identical, demonstrating the benefit of combining mental training with physical training. Beckham's results indicated that your brain cannot tell the difference between what is real and what is imagined when you give your visualisations enough detail and real sensory input. Therefore, by creating a vivid, clear picture in your mind of the way you want to perform, you can drastically improve your performance as the brain has already experienced the outcome you seek.

> They said I was too old but I did it. I had practised in my mind and saw myself do it.
>
> —Linford Christie, after winning gold in the 100 metre race at the Barcelona Olympics (1992) at the age of 32

If so many exceptionally successful people utilise these powerful techniques, why don't we all use them? Surely *our* goals are just as important! Our goal might not be to win an Olympic gold medal, but could visualisation work equally well for other goals we have?

The answer is, yes it can! By utilising the right approaches, you can breathe new life into your goals. No matter what goal you are pursuing, visualising yourself achieving it before you actually do can be a very positive step. Visualisation is the key that can unlock our true goal-achievement potential.

> Visualisation is daydreaming with a purpose.
>
> —Bo Bennett

Make the visualisation technique work for you

When performed correctly, visualisation can certainly yield powerful results. Why? Because when it comes time to act on the goals you've set for yourself, you will have already addressed the possible setbacks in your mind. More importantly, you will have already had the experience of succeeding.

In order to successfully implant your goal onto your subconscious mind, there are three steps that must be carried out:

1   Choose a goal-achievement 'moment' to focus on.

2   Decide precisely who or what is in your picture.

3   Imprint your vision onto your subconscious mind using either a simple visualisation or the time line technique.

Following is a detailed explanation of how to successfully implement these steps.

Choose a goal-achievement 'moment'

The first thing to do when preparing for a visualisation exercise is to choose one of the goals you've set using the POWERTIP system described in chapter 4. By this stage, you should have a few goals that you'd like to reach. Then, you're ready to implement the techniques of visualisation.

Choose a goal that you would like to embed into your subconscious mind for the year ahead. Think carefully about the final step in achieving that goal, the step that will result in you knowing that your goal has been achieved. Table 8.1 shows examples of specific 'moments' that could represent the achievement of a goal.

Table 8.1: visualising the achievement of your goals

Goal area	Key moment to visualise
Saving $100 000	The exact moment you see the money in your online bank account. Alternatively, it might be calling the bank for an account balance.
Walking to base camp on Mount Everest	The final few steps before reaching the destination.
Travelling to a favourite holiday destination	The moment you pick up the airline tickets: what would it feel like to have tickets in your hands for the first time?

Table 8.1 *(cont'd)*: visualising the achievement of your goals

Goal area	Key moment to visualise
Receiving a big promotion at work	The moment when the boss shakes your hand as he or she offers you the promotion.
Getting married	The moment when that special someone says 'I do'.

Whatever your goal, and whatever moment you choose to focus on for the purposes of the visualisation exercise, thinking about the final step should make you feel excited and increase the level of motivation you feel about reaching the goal you have set.

Decide precisely who or what is in your picture

For optimum results, it's best to try and engage *all* of your senses when visualising the moment you achieve your goals—so you not only see, but hear and feel yourself achieving the goal. This heightened clarity in your mind gives you increased confidence to succeed, which moves your desired outcome from the realm of possibility to probability—and then into the realm of reality.

> Imagination is the beginning of creation.
>
> —George Bernard Shaw

When constructing the mental image of achieving your goal, try and answer the following questions about your vision to ensure that your mental picture is as clear and powerful as it possibly can be.

▫ What colours are in your mental picture? Colour engages the creative side of the brain. Many studies demonstrate that colour can improve recall and motivation. Be sure to imbue your mental images with bright colours—and lots of them!

▫ What noises can you hear? These could be anything from a crowd cheering, your partner saying congratulations, wedding bells or the whirr of the computer as you look at an email or an account balance. If you are listening to someone speak, be careful to hear positive statements only. Take out any words that could indicate doubt or negativity. The words have to be simple and definite. Following are some examples of statements you could incorporate into your visualisation:

  • 'Congratulations, you've been appointed our new CEO!'

  • 'Excellent choice madam! Here are the keys to your blue Audi sports.'

  • 'Jim, you are now 25 kilograms lighter—and in only nine months! Well done.'

▫ Are there any smells or tastes that you are aware of? These could be anything from the smell of perfume, smoke from a start gun or the taste of wedding cake.

❑   How do you feel? List the emotions that you feel having achieved your goal. Some common emotions are pride, happiness and satisfaction.

Make the picture as clear and realistic as possible in your mind. You are determining what your *reality* (what you will see, hear and feel) will be like at the moment when you achieve your goal. When you see it realistically, it will stop being a dream and become the seed in your subconscious that leads to the future you want.

> I am the greatest; I said that even before I knew I was.
>
> —Muhammad Ali

Imprint your vision onto your subconscious mind

Once you have a strong vision of your moment of success, you can learn how to paint that picture into your subconscious brain with optimal results. There are two effective ways to do this: the vivid visualisation technique and the time line technique.

The vivid visualisation technique

Simple visualisation can be done anywhere, and for any length of time. It works best with regular repetition. Learning to visualise effectively can take time, and is easier for some people than others. Either way, it is well worth the perseverance.

Follow the steps described in the next section for maximum results:

1 *Relax the mind*. Without getting too technical, there are four major brain states: delta, theta, alpha and beta. Delta is the deep sleep state; theta is the daydream state; alpha is the relaxed awake state; and beta is the state of consciously engaged mental activity. Stress, worry and other negative emotions as well as peak concentration are experienced in this state. Visualisation is best done in a theta state where your mind is free to be creative and is open to suggestion. However, many people visualise well in alpha state too. So how do you best achieve a 'peak relaxation/visualisation state'? The answer will vary for each of us: you might play certain music, meditate, have a bath or relax on the sofa. The key is to minimise distraction and have no major 'to-do' item playing on your mind, otherwise your mind will remain in beta state. Similarly, if you plan to do a quick visualisation before bed, I suggest not reading the latest John Grisham book beforehand, because beta brain waves will be stimulated, making it difficult to be in the creative realm and picture your goal without distraction. Decide how you are going to regularly find the alpha or theta state; choose what suits you best and allow the time for it on a consistent basis.

2 *Summon the mental image you've developed into your mind*. This can require clarity, consistency, emotion and duration. The clearer you can make the picture

in your mind, the better. If it is a vivid picture, it will have a greater effect on you. Don't worry if it is not too clear to begin with; it can take some time before the picture becomes more defined, and if you are not used to visualising your skills will improve with practice. It may take you a few seconds to picture it clearly; for others it might take a few minutes. Infusing your visualisation picture with positive emotion is important. It makes the picture come alive with energy and vibrance, making you even more determined to achieve the goals that you have set.

3   *Repeat the process on a regular basis.* As it only takes a short period of time, I suggest visualising your goal achievement at least once a week. A great time to do this is just before bed or first thing in the morning.

Vision poster

A valuable visualisation aid is a vision poster. This device is a poster-sized picture designed to remind you of the exact goal you will be achieving. It can help to keep you motivated and inspired in times of uncertainty and doubt.

To make the most of the vision poster, choose a picture that acts as a powerful visual reminder of your goal and put it somewhere prominent where you will look on a regular basis. You might put it on the fridge, in the front of your diary or perhaps on the wall of your garage. If your goal is to get a new car, a picture of the exact car you want pinned up on a wall would be brilliant. You could improve on this by noting down in big letters on the picture the exact (realistic) date you will have this car. Personally I have used this technique year after year to great effect.

When putting together a vision poster, there are a couple of important things to consider:

▫ Choose a picture that closely resembles your goal. For example, if you want a car, the picture should reflect your preferred result (preferred colour, style, size and model). I often get asked where to look for the right picture. There are plenty of websites that sell or provide libraries of images. One that I have used in the past is a free pictures website: <www.sxc.hu>. It has over 300 000 images to choose from.

▫ You should feel motivated and inspired by seeing the picture. If it doesn't do much for you, consider changing the picture.

▫ Your vision poster needs to be placed somewhere you will get to see it regularly.

▫ Make sure the picture is high resolution and a reasonable size. The bigger, brighter and clearer your picture, the better!

The time line technique

There is a more detailed type of visualisation that aims to embed your goal into your subconscious mind called the 'time line technique', and it has helped many people achieve their goals.

All our memories (from when we were born to the present day) can be stored on a time line of events whereby our mind records and stores memories. Such a time line enables us to know the difference between the past, the present and the future. We all have many significant moments on our time line, which have made us into the people we are today. There will be significant moments in the future that determine where we end up in life. Sometimes it can be worthwhile thinking about how different choices made at crucial moments in our lives would have changed things. We can't change the past, of course, but we can learn from it. By making better decisions, we can change our future time line towards a happy, more fulfilled one.

Here's how the time line technique works:

1   Relax your mind (see page 163 for a detailed explanation of how to do this).

2   Close your eyes and imagine you have moved out of your physical body, and are floating above it. The idea is to look down at yourself as you continue to rise higher into the air.

3   Now picture a time line forming of the past, present and the future. The past will include significant events in your life, from the time of your birth right up until your current age. I often ask my clients to float along the time line into the past, looking down from a distance at different events in their lives. You can fly down closer to the event, even *into* the event, seeing it through your own eyes. This way you can relive a positive experience you have had in the past. When it comes to negative or limiting experiences, it is often best to view them from a distance if there

is significant trauma involved. A trained time line therapist can assist you in removing any negative feelings that surround certain experiences. By looking at past events, sometimes important life lessons are revealed.

4   Now comes the part of the process most critical to your goals. By floating towards the present time and into the future, you can float above the final step in achieving your goal. By floating down closer to the event, you can see, hear and feel what it is like to achieve the goal. By looking along your time line from that significant moment (of goal achievement) towards present time, you can picture key goal-achievement steps being inserted into your time line. To best utilise this goal-achievement technique, I suggest you read the goal achievement time line script in the appendix on page 231.

Visualisation is a powerful goal-achievement enhancer. It is like any other skill—the more you practise, the more skilful you are likely to become. Regardless of the goal that you want to achieve, it can have a powerful effect both in your business and personal life.

Chapter 8

The triple P
effectiveness blueprint

Once your POWERTIP goals are written down, you've worked out potential obstacles and you've implanted your goals into your subconscious mind, you are ready to create an action plan and a strategy to implement your goals.

This is an area where many people become unstuck. Strategies and plans surrounding goals are often not as effective as they need to be. The right strategic plan can give you the blueprint for success in all areas of life.

To ensure the maximum chance of success, you'll need to first break down your goals into smaller pieces, with mini milestones spaced out evenly in the time leading up to your achievement date. This is an important step, because it will give you clarity on what you need to achieve in shorter time frames, making it easier to concentrate your efforts. For example, you might aim to be a grade four pianist in 12 months' time. The mini milestones would simply be the achievement of a new level of accreditation every three months.

Where possible, break down your goals into even smaller portions to give you greater clarity. It is empowering to know exactly what results you need to achieve each month and each week to keep you on track. Once you have broken down your goals into smaller, more manageable pieces, I suggest placing the smaller outcomes in your diary, whether that be paper based or electronic. I suggest using different colours to help distinguish between big quarterly goals and weekly ones. It is worth writing the goals somewhere else too for backup purposes.

The next step is the triple P effectiveness blueprint, a simple method for effectively planning the achievement of your goals. If POWERTIP is about goal setting, then the triple P effectiveness blueprint is all about goal *getting*. It is a system that will help you navigate the most effective course towards your goal. The triple P effectiveness model can be broken down as follows:

1   *Power plan*. List all possible options for moving towards the goal you seek. There are often also a number of different approaches you can take to reach your goals; the trick is to think laterally and write all these down.

2   *Power play*. By utilising key resources and attributes to maximise your goal-achievement advantage, you can discover better, more efficient options for

putting your plan (devised in step one) into action. Fresh plan-implementation ideas can certainly breathe new life into the way you approach your goals.

3   *Prioritise*. Once all options are listed, you will be able to evaluate each option in terms of effectiveness and efficiency (the cost associated with using valuable time, money and energy). This step will provide you with a simple way to organise your proposed action steps into a time line of events between the present day and goal-achievement time.

The way in which these elements interrelate to one another is depicted in figure 8.1.

Figure 8.1: the triple P effectiveness blueprint

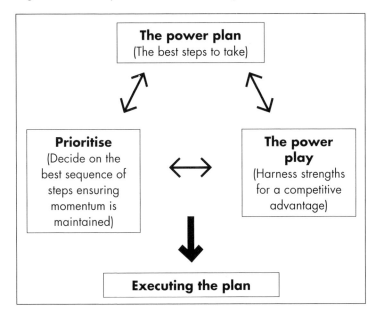

Power plan

When I was at university, one of my professors told me the following piece of advice: 'One minute spent in effective planning saves 10 minutes in execution'. This advice turned out to be invaluable, and has since proved true on numerous occasions.

Many years ago, I was running late to see a client. With some urgency, I jumped in the car and took off without a glance at the road map. Within minutes, I had already taken a wrong turn and gone down a one-way street — the clock was ticking! I had to make a desperate phone call to the client to explain that I would be late. I thought I knew where to go and the best way to get there, but clearly I was wrong. If I had spent a few moments just doing the simple thing of looking at a map, it would have made all the difference.

Having been involved with numerous planning committees, I have seen the amount of time that goes to waste through poor planning. I have worked with managers who are 'serial planners.' They plan out their initial plans; get advice on what to do from anyone and everyone, and then eventually settle on a plan that does not deliver results anyway. I have flown interstate to attend planning meetings that were poorly organised from the outset! It is actually quite frightening how much time is wasted by a failure to plan properly.

Examples of poor planning can be found in every area of life. The following is a recent example of how time, money and energy can be wasted by poor planning. It relates to an Australian inner-city rail line, whose goal was to provide rail transportation between Epping and Chatswood. Poor planning resulted in a disastrous outcome that wasted millions of dollars and enormous amounts of time. Already running behind construction deadlines, the first few train trips using the new tunnel were marked with resounding dissatisfaction when noise readings revealed that commuters would endure 85 decibels during the 15-minute journey (this is the equivalent of a Boeing 737 landing). This project's launch date was pushed back further when it was found that the quieter trains could not be used in the tunnel due to the overly steep gradient. Alternate trains were sourced but discarded because they were too old and didn't have air-conditioning, and were therefore in breach of commuter travel standards. Other trains were eventually found for use in this tunnel, but by then construction costs had almost doubled to $2.3 billion and the project was two years overdue!

Most plans examine only a few obvious options, after which decisions are made and the plan is formulated—a reasonable approach, but there is a better way that will take you to your goals faster.

So, how can you avoid disastrous outcomes such as this one? What is the most effective way to plan your actions when trying to reach your goal?

The simple answer is by thinking laterally and strategically about your planning, and completing it carefully and comprehensively. The power plan is more than a plan; it is a *structured* way of planning that encompasses all crucial ingredients that you should consider when mapping your goal-achievement route.

To understand the power plan, it is useful to think of a portable navigation system. If you type your destination in to the device, it automatically picks out the best route. But what factors does the device consider when deciding on the best route? Time efficiency? Fuel efficiency? Distance? Many navigation systems give the shortest distance as the default option. However, this does not always factor in road conditions or traffic delays such as the number of traffic lights, the flow of traffic or even the occasional crash. Imagine a navigation system that was able to analyse all this. Wouldn't that save you time!

Power planning is in some ways similar to creating your own internal navigation system—one that incorporates all the factors that could impact on your ability to reach your goals.

In order to create the best possible plan, ensure that you ask yourself quality questions. Rather than simply asking, 'What can I do to get me to my goal?' you should be asking, 'How am I going to achieve my goal in a way that best utilises my time, money and energy and other resources?'

To simplify the process, I have provided a breakdown of all the questions you'll need to answer in order to ensure maximum success when working out a power plan. These are discussed following.

Who can help and who can hinder my progress?

Knowing you have people you can call on in tough times gives you reassurance and confidence for the challenges goal-achievement brings. Similarly, inspirational people can give you added drive to complete your tasks.

Importantly, having a friend or relative who holds you accountable creates an added incentive to stick to your plans and carry out the tasks you've set for yourself. It's like always having a life-saving vest or 'get out of jail free' card up your sleeve.

Sadly, there are some people who act knowingly or unknowingly like a virus (not just purely in regard to your goals, but to your life in general). They are the cynics, critics, killjoys and naysayers whose negative words can infiltrate your achievement mindset, creating doubt. They might make cutting comments such as the following:

- 'You can't do that!'

- 'Why do you bother?'

- 'As if you have any chance really of achieving your goal.'

If you know these people have a negative effect on you, avoiding them—or at least avoiding the demoralising conversations—is very worthwhile!

In order to ensure you have these 'life jackets' when you actualise your plans, and that you don't have toxic energy preventing you from maintaining your inspiration levels, it is useful to ask yourself the following questions:

- Who can I learn from?

- Who can support me and my goals?

- Who can inspire me?

- Who will hold me accountable for sticking to my goals and deadlines?

❑ Who are the people I need to avoid? (The critics, naysayers and cynics.)

At the end of this step, you should have a list of people who can help you achieve your goals. I suggest also making a list of people you may wish to avoid having goal conversations with, as they are likely to bring down your self-confidence.

What do I need to learn?

Achieving your goals does not just happen; it takes a lot of hard work! The Japanese work philosophy of Kaizen, meaning continuous improvement, has never been more important than today. Enhancing your skills and expanding your résumé are the best ways to ensure you stay a valuable commodity in today's competitive labour market. Knowledge and skill development are significantly more valuable when practically applied. I knew a PhD graduate who worked in a high-powered job for more than 20 years, only to find himself suddenly without work. His unwillingness to expand and update his skills meant years of unemployment before he eventually found another job. I think that the best investment you can make is undoubtedly in yourself, because no matter what happens in the competitive job market, progressive, current skills are always in demand.

 Blake's TIP To have more, you must be more.
To be more, you must do more.
To do more, you must learn more.

While I was working with some top sales people in Melbourne, a retail manager shared with me his goal of having the highest performing retail jewellery store in Australia within three years (there were 100 stores in the company). He defined 'high performing' in terms of earning the highest revenue. He was very determined to achieve this goal, and there was real fire in his eyes as he said it. I asked him what he needed to learn to make this goal a reality. He wasn't quite sure how to answer — in fact, he hadn't thought about it at all. His answer was: 'I need to learn the best strategies used by the best retailers'.

I told the man that his answer was a good start, but in order to succeed in his quest he would need to identify more specific key result areas (KRAs). In other words, the man needed to discover what *precise results* he needed to achieve in the major retail performance areas. Specifically, he would need to find out what results had been achieved by the current top store on a number of different performance parameters such as sales, customer service, store layout, incidence of theft, staff turnover, profit ratio and so on. By communicating with the company's head office, or perhaps with a regional manager, the man would be able to get all the information he needed.

This valuable information would give the retail manager the clarity he needed on the kind of results required to achieve his goal. He would then be able to compare his own store's recent results with those achieved by the premier store. By knowing what the top store is already achieving in each key results area, he would be in a much better position to write down his key learning areas — the knowledge and skills needed to achieve those same results as the top store. For example, the retail manager might have discovered that the store needed to sell more to each customer; to expand the stock range; or to improve their average customer spend.

Too often people learn things that are useful rather than critical. It is important to know what you *need* to learn in order to reach the goals you seek. That way you can discover the best way to acquire the relevant knowledge or skills.

Once you have decided on your key learning areas, you need to discover what options are available to help you gain the skills and knowledge you need. You can best fill the gaps in your key learning areas by answering the following questions.

- ❑   What do I need to learn? (Specifically, what knowledge and skills would be beneficial?)

- ❑   Who has already achieved what I hope to achieve? How might I be able to learn from them?

- ❑   What resources will help? (These might consist of books, audio programs, mentors, training programs, university courses and online courses.)

- ❑   What will the resources cost me?

- ❑   Are the resources worthwhile?

- ❑   What can you put into place to ensure you maintain motivation and momentum?

After completing this step, you should have a good understanding of exactly which areas need to be improved, and exactly what you need to do in order to learn the skills you'll need to reach your goals. You can decide on which key learning areas will be of most benefit to you by researching the key results achieved by others with similar goals.

How do I get there?

Keeping in mind your answers to the questions you answered about who can help and hinder, and what resources you'll need, you now need to write down all the steps that can take you closer to your goal.

List *all* the possible steps that will help you achieve your goals, and write down time frames next to them. It is a good idea to list 10 or 20 possible steps that you can take. Some of these steps can be completely ridiculous! Particularly if your goal is complex and could benefit from some lateral thinking, listing a few completely outlandish options might be just what you need to shake things up a bit. The process of listing seemingly ridiculous options stimulates some right brain creativity that could be beneficial to you in terms of coming up with the best possible action plan.

One senior manager I worked with was struggling to meet his work targets. I asked him to write me a list of things that he could do to increase the performance of his team. He came up with a list of five points, and said that he had already been doing some of these things without a great deal of success. I asked him who he had shared this list with. The answer was 'no-one'; he was relying entirely on his own solutions to the problem. I asked the manager what he would do if none of the activities were an option. 'Panic', he joked.

I then asked him if he could come up with at least 20 new approaches to his problem. He looked at me bewildered until I explained that 10 of the 20 approaches could be totally ridiculous; in fact, the more ridiculous the better! The manager agreed to complete the task and to get feedback on the approaches from at least two other people whom he knew, liked and trusted.

Within a month, the manager had completely turned his team around as a result of implementing one of the suggestions on his piece of paper.

It never hurts to get some new perspectives on your goal steps. When writing down possible actions that will bring you closer to your goal, ask the following questions:

- What are *all* the possible steps I can take? (The more you write, the better!)

- What tasks can fast-track the path to my goals?

- Whom can I ask for feedback on my proposed action steps?

For example, if your goal were to reach a target weight of 65 kilograms, you might write the following steps on your list:

- walk up and down the stairs at work instead of using the lift

- buy a pedometer that counts the number of steps walked in a day; set a daily target

- eat more fruit and vegetables and less processed, fatty foods

- buy a bike.

Some steps that could fast track your progress would be:

◻ perform high-repetition resistance training four times a week

◻ ask a friend to be your training partner

◻ drink at least one glass of water every time you feel hungry

◻ eat a breakfast high in complex carbohydrates and protein.

And the list could go on for pages. You might even ask friends or relatives if they can think of any other steps that might help you achieve what you want; external perspectives can be surprisingly illuminating.

At the end of this step you should have a comprehensive list of possible actions that you could take in order to move you closer to your goal.

Power play

The power play in goal achievement is about utilising strengths and taking new, innovative approaches to get to your goals faster.

I love the idea of learning from those who have already achieved the results I want to achieve, but sometimes what worked for someone else will not work for you. This could be the case for a few different reasons, including the following:

◻ your knowledge, skill level and personality might be different from those of the person you are learning from

- what worked in another country, state or local community may not work in your location

- you might find that a strategy that was successful in the past is now outdated, and overrun by technological advancement and changing societal needs.

There are often better approaches to reach your goals, but only if you are really looking for them. It's like being so used to getting a plane from London to Paris that you don't realise that the Eurail (fast train) usually works out to be faster, simpler and cheaper. Perhaps there are faster, simpler and cheaper ways to reach your goals that you haven't thought of yet.

The success of Brazilian entrepreneur Ricardo Semler is a perfect example. In 1980 at the age of 21, Semler convinced his father to stand down as CEO of the engineering company Semco, to allow him, Ricardo, to assume the role. Ricardo Semler turned the management of the company upside down, firing 60 per cent of the managers and slowly but surely placing management into the hands of the employees. He introduced a unique approach of self-governance, treating employees as adults. Employees were given shares in the company and decided on their own working conditions—they even set their own wages!

Semler managed to increase Semco's revenue from $4 million in 1982 to over $200 million in 2003. The company thrived during the tough early 1990s when the majority of construction businesses in Brazil went under.

With the breakneck speed of technological advancement, it is more important than ever to have forward, innovative thinking.

Gaining an advantage in going for your goals sometimes requires a new way of seeing the same thing. You need to be able to think outside the square, to come up with new strategies and approaches to help you achieve results from time to time. It certainly can stretch the brain's capacity, which is never a bad thing!

There are a number of things you can do to make it easier to think innovatively around possible goal achievement steps, including the following:

▫ Never judge ideas — *any* idea is a good idea. (It isn't until the next stage that you work out what steps are the right ones to take.)

▫ Have some relaxing background music playing while coming up with ideas, especially baroque music (pieces by Bach, Handel or Vivaldi are particularly helpful).

▫ Alter your physical environment while you write. For example, you might choose to write possible steps while relaxing in a hot bath (not recommended at work!) or brainstorm ideas outside in the fresh air.

▫ Use a mind map to visually represent new options coming from existing ones. The idea is to have the result you are looking to achieve in a box in the middle of the page, and then a series of branches coming off it. Branches can then extend from other branches, creating a free-flowing network of ideas and options.

Another great way to enhance the power play part of the blueprint is to harness your unique talents and abilities where possible. If you are able to find activities that you are skilled at, enjoy doing and which are highly valuable, then you have struck goal-achievement gold. For example, a number of years ago I utilised my unique ability to do impressions of famous actors to help me achieve my public speaking goals. It was not an obvious step to take, but an approach that truly fast tracked my success.

By the end of the power play step, you should have some new innovative steps towards achieving your goals. Ideally you have also listed your unique strengths and have included some steps that best utilise your abilities.

Prioritise

Many people struggle to select and prioritise goal-achievement activities; they spend too much money, invest too much time or select activities that are painstaking to complete. Selecting the best steps to take in the right sequence is a skill in itself, but one that we can all develop with a bit of practice.

For each potential activity listed in the power plan section, ask the following important questions:

▫ How much time will it take?

▫ What will it cost? (if applicable)

▫ How effective is the task in moving you closer towards the goal?

▫ Will you enjoy doing the task?

These questions help you decide which activities are the 'must do' activities to move you closer to your goals. You should consider your individual values and priorities when deciding which tasks will work best for you. The exercise in table 3.1 can help you evaluate each option with clarity.

By using a tool I refer to as the four quadrant model of momentum (see figure 8.2 below), you will be able to effectively prioritise the tasks you will need to undertake in order to achieve your goals.

Figure 8.2: the four quadrant model of momentum

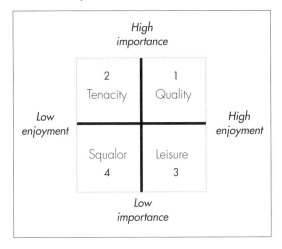

The vertical axis of the quadrant measures how important the activity is to the achievement of your goal. The higher the reading, the more impact the activity will have in moving you closer to your goal. For example, if your goal were to save $10 000, you might find that investing in certain stocks is of higher importance than buying an investment property, due to the current economic climate. Therefore, investing would be positioned higher up on the vertical axis.

The horizontal axis measures enjoyment. If you enjoy doing a particular activity, it will fall on the right side of the axis; if you don't enjoy the activity, it will appear on the left. For example, if your goal were to improve your relationship by making your partner feel special on his or her birthday, you might find that taking him or her on a surprise weekend away might be more enjoyable than organising a surprise party. Both options would be on competing sides of the horizonal axis.

Once you've plotted your activity on each axis, you'll notice that it will fall into one of the four quadrants. The quadrants, in order of desirability and effectiveness, represent the following:

- Quadrant one: quality

- Quadrant two: tenacity

- Quadrant three: leisure

- Quadrant four: squalor.

I will now discuss each quadrant in greater detail.

Quadrant one is the quadrant of quality—the quadrant of choice for potential goal-getting activities; you enjoy what you are doing, and are getting a great return on your efforts, which are elevating you in the direction of your goal. It tends to be easy to maintain momentum towards your goals when your activities fall into this quadrant. If only all goal-getting activities were in this quadrant!

Quadrant two is the tenacity quadrant, and is very much the engine room that moves you towards the goal you seek. You may not enjoy the activities you do in this quadrant, but you understand that they help lead you to where you want to go. The 'no pain, no gain' philosophy was born here. If you spend too much time in this quadrant, your motivation can seriously drop.

Quadrant three includes activities that you enjoy doing, but have little importance to the goals you are pursuing. Examples of this might include emailing or tweeting friends; having an extended lunch break; or playing the latest game on your mobile phone. Activities that fall inside this quadrant are enjoyable but unproductive.

Quadrant four refers to activities that are neither important nor enjoyable. Why would anyone spend any time in this area? It doesn't make a great deal of sense, but you would be surprised how many people do exactly that. In a business sense, you might go to a meeting which is not enjoyable and is also a huge time waster; you might answer unwanted phone calls; respond to useless email requests; and waste time looking for things that you have misplaced.

If you plot all the steps needed to reach your goals on the four quadrant model, you will notice how many of those tasks are in quadrant two or quadrant one (the most desirable quadrants). If there is an even spread of the two areas, you might consider interspersing quadrant three activities with the quadrant one activities to help you maintain momentum.

From a momentum standpoint, it can be very difficult to keep your motivational drive going if you are constantly doing quadrant two activities. When I was studying financial accounting as part of my postgraduate degree, I was constantly doing quadrant two activities. I had to pass the subject to stay on track with my studies, but found it really difficult to get motivated. I'm sure you can relate to a time when you had to work really hard to get yourself to follow through with action. So how might you boost the activity from quadrant two and turn it into a quadrant one activity? Here are some tips:

- Make the task more enjoyable by changing your mindset. Perhaps you can find greater meaning by realising that any mental challenge makes your mind stronger and better prepared for future challenges.

- Make the activity more fun. For one really difficult assignment, I decided to make a friendly competition with some fellow students. Even though the subject wasn't of great interest to me, the challenge of beating my friends was!

- Have some quadrant three activities at the ready to break up the flow. That way, you are taking valuable time out on occasion to recharge the batteries for the next attack run in quadrant two.

Even if you struggle to move tenacity quadrant activities all the way across into quadrant one, you still might have luck making it more enjoyable. For example, you might not enjoy exercising at all, but perhaps watching your favourite show while running on a treadmill will help you reach your target weight in a way that is a bit more fun. Perhaps you could exercise with a good friend to make the experience a social one at the same time. If you are really likely to get through some of the important, unenjoyable tasks, perhaps you can delegate them to others or get some help. Perhaps your energy is best used elsewhere.

Blake's TIP   Powerful planning prevents poor performance.

By the end of the third phase of the triple P effectiveness regime, you should have prioritised the best action steps you can take towards your goals, thus giving you an indication of the best actions to lead you to your goals. By plotting actions in the four quadrant model of momentum, you can begin to see how you might divide tasks in the time leading up to your goal deadline to give you enhanced momentum.

The triple P effectiveness regime is there to empower you and to keep you motivated and on track to reach your goals. Remember the three Ps: power plan, power play and prioritise. If you've completed the exercises discussed in this chapter, you should be in a great position to execute your plans and achieve your goals for the year ahead.

Chapter 9

Maintaining momentum: executing the plan

By this stage in the book, you should have progressed significantly in your journey to set and achieve goals that reflect your values. You should have correctly formulated your goals using the POWERTIP system; learnt to visualise a vivid picture of your goals in your mind; and mapped out the action steps needed to achieve the goals you've set. It is now time to execute the plan.

Achieving the goals that you've set will be about building and maintaining momentum.

Motivation and momentum are closely linked. The word 'motivation' comes from the Latin word *motere*, which means 'to take action' and refers to something or someone that drives you to act. Momentum, on the other hand, is the impetus gained by a moving object. Therefore, it makes sense that momentum is gained by the maintenance of motivation over time. To achieve your goals, momentum is critical.

Goals are useless without proper execution. It is not uncommon for people to be fired up about a goal initially, and then lose motivation and momentum somewhere along the way. Once the motivation flame has been extinguished, it can take some real effort to set it alight again.

> There is a difference between knowing
> the path and walking the path.
>
> —Morpheus, *The Matrix*

We all lose motivation and drive from time to time — it is part of being human. Occasionally, we just won't feel excited, energetic and happy. Some motivational speakers preach that we can be happy all the time, but I don't believe such an expectation is realistic. It is human nature to go through a range of emotions, and perhaps we need to spend some time in a low emotional state because of life circumstances such as the death of a loved one, a relationship breakdown or being retrenched from work. If you had a bad day at work, it is only natural to feel a bit tired and dejected as a result.

Having said that, I do believe that we can improve our state of mind in an instant by doing positive things such as shifting our attention; focusing on something positive; changing our posture; putting a smile on our dial; or physically moving our bodies. The important thing is to understand that we are in control of when we choose to move out of that negative state.

It is important to allow ourselves to experience different emotional states, because each one carries with it a message that we can learn from. Generally, if we engage with our emotions, we can benefit from:

▫ being in the present and understanding why we feel the way we do

▫ changing our focus because we deem our emotional response to be unhealthy or unwarranted

▫ understanding what triggered the emotional state in the first place. There is usually a lesson to be learnt.

How you feel is just one of the core ingredients that can help you build and maintain momentum towards your goals. As I have not found a good model for maintaining momentum, I spent a great deal of time researching the key ingredients that help people to stay motivated towards their goals. The simple yet powerful model I have developed is the FIVESTAR model of momentum.

You might now be thinking, 'not another acronym!', and you're right — this book has a handful of them. But there is a good reason for this. I love Stephen Covey's *The 7 Habits of Highly Effective People*, but most people will only remember three or four of the habits discussed in the book after they finish reading it. Acronyms are brilliant because they make it easier to remember larger units of information. Table 9.1 (overleaf) depicts the FIVESTAR model of momentum.

Table 9.1: Beattie's FIVESTAR model of momentum

Fun	If something is enjoyable, it is so much easier to maintain motivation. To keep momentum going, consider doing one of the following things: • change the activities you're using to implement your goals • change the way you think about your goals • give yourself a fun reward for achieving smaller goals.
Inspiration	Daily doses of inspiration can give you the added boost you need to stay on target. The inspiration can come from a range of sources including the following: • books • audio tapes • seminars • quotes • other people.
Vision	Visual reminders of our goals can be a great way of maintaining momentum. Your visual reminder could be in a number of forms, including the following: • calendars, where you tick off successes • key pictures • charts • vivid visualisations, where you see yourself achieving your goal and the positive difference it makes to your life.
Energy	Without the requisite energy levels, it is hard to maintain any kind of momentum. An abundance of energy provides the fuel required to complete the tasks needed to achieve our goals.

S upport	The right kind of support can keep you accountable, motivated and on track. Ideally, surround yourself with positive people who will encourage you as well as hold you accountable.
T racking	Review your goals regularly, and update them as needed. Tracking includes changing your approach if you are off track, and in some cases shifting the goal posts.
A ction	Taking any positive action in the direction of your goals can help you maintain momentum, no matter how small that action might be. It's the little things done regularly that keep the momentum wheel spinning.
R ewards	Knowing that something truly worthwhile awaits you after you've achieved your intended goal can be a great motivator. Similarly, it can be beneficial to reward each significant goal milestone achieved along the way to final goal.

So how do you use the FIVESTAR model?

You can use the FIVESTAR model in two ways: when your momentum train has been derailed, it can be used to get you back on track; and it can be used as a tool throughout the entire goal-achievement journey to keep you on task and on time.

Let's take a look at each aspect of the system in more detail, so you know how best to implement what I refer to as 'momentum moments'.

Fun

One great way to maintain momentum towards your goals is to make the achievement of your goals fun. The more you enjoy what you do, the easier it will be to take action. If only every step along your goal achievement path was enjoyable!

If you have an important goal task to complete that you don't enjoy doing, you have a couple of options.

- *Change your thoughts.* Sometimes you can change the way you think about the activity or task that can make it more enjoyable. For example, you could focus on the benefits rather than the pain involved. For tips on overcoming procrastination, see chapter 5.

- *Delegate some of the tasks required to reach the goal to others.* Enlist help to complete the task or at least help you with it (if possible). For example, if you dread completing financial reports, you could entrust someone else to finish them for you. You can then free up your energy to do other important things.

- *Change your task.* Perhaps there is another way to progress towards your goals that is more enjoyable, but that has similar results. For example, if you aim to lose weight but hate going to the gym, you might consider joining the local soccer team, or investing in a bike.

Blake's TIP If it's fun, it's not hard to get it done.

The four quadrant theory of momentum in chapter 8 might be helpful in managing your tasks for greater momentum.

Inspiration

It's amazing how hearing the right thing at the right time can lift the spirits and breathe new life into your goal-seeking endeavours. Little bits of inspiration can help keep you focused on your goal. So where can you get the inspiration from? Some suggestions are listed following:

- motivational speakers

- books

- audio programs

- friends

- family

- work colleagues

- quotes (consider buying a quote calendar)

- YouTube

- DVDs

- inspiring emails.

And the list goes on. The trick is to find what inspires you, and have it easily accessible when you need it most.

For example, you might have your favourite motivational audio program ready to listen to in the car on the way to work. Alternatively, you might spend five minutes before you start each work day watching an inspiring YouTube video or reading an inspiring story.

Vision

It can be difficult to maintain one's focus on a goal if the end destination seems far away. Harnessing visual stimuli can help you maintain momentum. Some examples of how to incorporate visual stimuli into your quest to stay motivated include:

- putting an inspiring picture in a prominent place (on the fridge or mirror, or as a screensaver on your computer screen)

- creating a movie in your mind about the final goal-achievement step, and the positive difference it makes to you. Have a clear picture of what you would see, hear and feel when you have achieved your goal. This simple visualisation works best when you are in a relaxed state (see chapter 7 for more information)

- having a meaningful quote with a message placed in a worthwhile spot. For instance, I have the words *carpe diem* displayed on my computer, which remind me to make each day count

- ticking off your mini goals and milestones on a large poster, which is a great visual cue.

> ## Vision is the art of seeing the invisible.
>
> —Helen Keller

Energy

Without mental and physical energy, it is very hard to maintain any real kind of momentum towards your goals. There are four main ways to change your energy levels: good nutrition, exercise, rest and recreation, and changing your mood.

Nutrition

Eating the right foods and drinking enough water can make a big difference to your energy levels. To have plenty of energy to achieve your goals, it is important to:

- eat smaller meals throughout the day (six smaller meals instead of three big meals is best)

- drink eight glasses of water a day

- have a diet high in fibre, protein and carbohydrates and low in fat, sugar and salt.

If you are feeling low in energy, remember to ask yourself the following questions:

- Does your diet allow for maximum energy?

- Where can you improve your nutrition to provide greater energy levels?

There is often a simple solution to the problem.

Exercise

How fit and healthy are you?

If you are carrying around a bit of excess weight or lack physical fitness, your energy levels will suffer. Some people talk about how great it would be having an extra hour each day to get things done. Having increased energy levels is like having an extra hour, because you will be far more productive in the time you have at your disposal. I suggest finding an exercise buddy and finding a form of exercise you enjoy doing.

Rest and recreation

Getting enough rest and reducing unnecessary stress are important factors in recharging the batteries. If you are all 'go go go' towards your goals, you risk burning out. Aim to get around eight hours of sleep a night, and take regular vacations during the year to relax and unwind. Taking time out from the hustle and bustle of everyday life makes a difference. By not taking my phone or laptop on a recent holiday, I was able to spend a priceless few days relaxing by the water, reading my book and lying in a hammock. On my return I was completely recharged and it showed in the quality of work I was able to produce. It was exactly what I needed.

Changing your mood

Your feelings and emotions play a big part in your energy and motivation levels. Too many people feel average at best for fair chunks of the day, but never do anything about it.

An elder Cherokee Native American was
teaching his grandchildren about life.

He said to them, 'A fight is going on inside
me. It is a terrible fight, and it is between two
wolves. One wolf represents fear, anger, envy,
sorrow, regret, greed, spite, arrogance, self-pity,
guilt, resentment, inferiority, lies, false pride,
superiority, ego and unfaithfulness.

'The other wolf stands for joy, peace, love, hope,
sharing, serenity, humility, kindness, forgiveness,
integrity, benevolence, friendship, empathy,
generosity, truth, compassion and faithfulness.

'This same fight is going on inside you,
and inside every other person too.'

They thought about it for a minute then one child
asked his grandfather, 'Which wolf will win?'

The old Cherokee simply replied, 'The one you feed'.

—Anonymous

There are four helpful ways to change how you feel at any
one time:

1   *Change your thoughts:* Any time you feel bad, sad,
    depressed, angry or frustrated you are focused
    on something negative. Therefore, if you want
    to change how you feel, shift your focus. At any
    moment, you can change how you feel by shifting
    your focus—so why don't we do that when we
    feel bad? It is usually out of habit that we stay in a
    negative emotional state longer than we need to.
    Just like a TV channel, if you don't like what is on,

you can change the station to something that you would prefer to watch. The same applies in our minds. If you are focusing on something that is depressing and negative, you only need to change the station (or focal point) and you can shift your whole emotional state. Bringing how you are feeling to conscious awareness is the first step to change.

2   *Change your physicality:* Due to the connection between mind and body, changing body posture can make a significant difference to how you feel. By standing tall, smiling and having your shoulders back, you tend to feel more empowered and positive.

3   *Change your actions*: It is much harder to feel bad when you are moving. Movement creates energy in the body and gets oxygen in the blood flowing. Aerobic exercise can also produce mood elevating hormones that are more powerful than morphine. Going for a run, hitting a punching bag or swimming in a pool are just some examples of things you can do to change how you feel.

4   *Change your environment*: Certain environments can make a significant difference to your mood. For example, you might go outside for some fresh air to lift your spirits during a busy day at work. Or if one venue gets you down, you could change the lighting, music, desk or wall colours. Perhaps some inspiring pictures can give you the mood lift you need each day.

Support

Having the right supporters around you can make a big difference to maintaining your momentum. Just think of a major sporting event where the local team has the encouragement of thousands of raving fans. Some amazing sporting performances were made possible because the right support lifted the performance of the athlete(s). The same applies when going for your goals. Certain people will offer you great support along the way if you ask them for it. (See the resilience section in chapter 5 for further details).

Enlist the help of an accountability buddy

A great momentum tool is to utilise an accountability buddy—someone who knows your goals and who holds you accountable. When choosing an accountability buddy, it is important that you know, like, respect and trust him or her. It is important that he or she is not too sympathetic of excuses, and can challenge you if you are not on track. Ideally, he or she would contact you regularly (around each mini milestone or sub-goal at a minimum) to check your progress. The accountability buddy could also hold the key to your rewards, making sure you only receive rewards when you have earned them.

Tracking

Watching two of the world's best tennis players going head to head at Wimbledon would be a wonderful spectacle, but what if we changed it up a bit so there was no scoreboard and the umpire was not allowed to announce the game or set score. It certainly would be a bit different if you had no idea of who was winning the contest. Knowing the updated score is a great feedback mechanism that is important in maintaining momentum, and it doesn't just apply to sport. Knowing exactly how you are faring en route to your goals in any life area is worthwhile, whether it be in your career, health or key relationships. By tracking your progress, you can see if you are meeting your daily and weekly targets on a consistent basis.

 Blake's TIP People tend to be far more productive when they are keeping score.

At least once a week, you should keep track of where you are at with your goals. The process of successful tracking goes like this:

❑ *Review*: Are you on track? Have you achieved the outcomes you wanted over the past week? Why / Why not?

❑ *Re-engineer the plan*: What will you do differently next week (if anything)? Decide on the actions you will take in the coming week that will move you closer towards your goal.

Action

A sprinter will be able to make up considerable ground in a small time frame, but will then run out of puff. Marathon runners are able to go much greater distances as a result of their consistent efforts. Going too hard too early can be dangerous for your goal-achievement chances. The classic case of this is someone going to the gym for the first time in years and working really hard. They are then so sore afterwards that they don't go back to the gym! Taking small, consistent action steps is a great way of maintaining momentum.

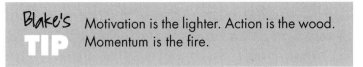

Blake's TIP Motivation is the lighter. Action is the wood. Momentum is the fire.

Motivation gives you the impetus to begin, but it is via regular, repeated actions that you can gain momentum. I suggest getting into the habit of planning your goal-getting actions on a weekly basis and executing the plan. Taking positive actions (no matter how big or small) can help you keep the inner fire going for longer towards your goals. (Chapter 8 can help you choose the right actions towards your goals.)

Rewards

Setting a rewards system can be a great source of motivation. It surprises me how few people set up a good rewards system for themselves. When you have reached a milestone on your way to achieving your goal, reward yourself. It gives you a feeling of achievement. The important thing when coming up with the right rewards is that you only reward yourself when you have actually achieved your milestones. Better still, have someone you can trust be in charge of the rewards (see the section on accountability buddies on page 203). That way they can ensure that you *only* receive the reward if you reach your target.

For example, if your goal is to reach your target weight by a certain date, you can choose a worthwile reward at each critical milestone. You might decide to reward yourself at the quarter, half and three quarter marks when you achieve your outcome. As a reward, I wouldn't suggest eating at your favourite all-you-can-eat buffet though. Instead you may choose to reward yourself with a weekend away, a massage or tickets to see a show you'd love to see.

The rewards must be a motivating force for you and be something you *really* want.

Having read this chapter, you should have the tools needed to maintain momentum. I would suggest reading this chapter a couple of times, and then teaching it to someone else. By doing this, you ensure that you understand and remember each of the key points. Whenever you feel like your momentum is slipping, I suggest looking at the FIVESTAR model to help you become motivated once again.

 Blake's TIP Momentum is the next day's tour de force. It helps you start from a high to launch even higher.

Chapter 10

The magic mindset in goal achievement

The human mind is a treasure chest of dreams, but many people have misplaced the key to unlock it. This chapter is about finding that key and then unlocking the true potential of your dreams. In this chapter, I examine the mindset of true champions, the belief-changing blueprint, and the secrets to retaining focus towards your goals. Once you have conquered the boundaries within, it becomes easier to break through the external boundaries.

The power of the mind

What lies between your ears is the most powerful super-computer in the world, so it makes sense to harness its energy towards the achievement of your goals. To explain exactly how powerful the human mind is, allow me to cite some extraordinary facts about the physiological workings of the brain.

The estimated storage capacity of the brain is said to be around a petabyte (the equivalent to a thousand terabytes of information—around 10 billion encyclopedia pages). Information can travel inside the brain at a speed of 120 metres per second—faster than the speed of sound. Our brain does over four million calculations every second. It would take the best computer of today a century to do what our brain does in one minute.

To further illustrate the power of our mind in manifesting goals, there are two areas of science that are worth examining, namely neuroplasticity and the placebo effect. Let's start with the placebo effect.

The placebo effect and goal achievement

Doctors have prescribed medicine to cure ailments for centuries, but more recent research suggests that the medicine itself might not always be what actually cures the patient. In recent times, experts have been asking the following question: is it the actual medicine that helps restore our health, or is it our belief about what that medicine will do for us?

The placebo effect refers to the beneficial effect experienced by a patient following treatment that arises from the patient's expectations concerning the treatment, rather than from the treatment itself. In other words, certain procedures and medicines can be prescribed not so much for their *physical* benefits, but for the psychological ones.

In a landmark study in the US, six people with crippling knee pain were booked in to have knee arthroscopies to help their condition. Under a general anaesthetic, surgeons made three incisions in the front of the knees in all six patients. However, the extent of the treatment from that point on varied: two of the patients received the normal knee operation; two of the patients had only a minimal surgical intervention; and the last two had nothing done at all (just the incisions). The surgeons had pretended to do the whole knee operation on the last group. All six patients woke up with stitches along their knees, and assumed that a full operation had been performed.

The results? Before the knee operation (or lack thereof), all six patients had great difficulty walking due to severe knee pain. After the operation, all six patients experienced an amazing recovery. All six experienced the same amount of healing, and returned to pain-free knee movement.

The power of one's beliefs surrounding medication is clearly as powerful (if not more so) than the medication itself. In goal-achievement terms, this means that the belief you have about your chances of reaching your goals can play a big part in achieving your outcome. But more on that later; there is another incredible phenomenon that helps explain the importance of rewiring your thought patterns to maximise the chances of achieving your goals: neuroplasticity.

Neuroplasticity and goal achievement

Neuroplasticity literally means the ability of the brain (*neuro*) to change itself (*plasticity*). Neuroscientists believed for a long time that the brain was hardwired, but new research reveals that the human brain has a remarkable ability to rewire itself. Our thoughts, actions and environment can cause substantial changes in the brain, including a reorganisation of where specific brain functions are located. This is great news when it comes to goal achievement — it means that no matter what brain patterns we have running at a subconscious level, we can change them.

In his groundbreaking book *The Brain That Changes Itself*, Dr Norman Doidge gives some amazing examples of the brain's ability to rewire itself. A particularly fascinating example refers to a woman named Cheryl Schultz, whose body's sensory balancing system (vestibular apparatus) stopped working after taking medication that damaged her inner ear structure. This meant that she could no longer stand without falling over. If she turned her head, the whole room would spin. Most people with this disorder develop severe psychological disorders, and many commit suicide.

A team of biophysicists developed a construction style hat with a built-in accelerometer (movement sensor similar to those found in iPods and gaming machines). The hat was hooked up to a computer, and Cheryl was instructed to place a small plastic strip with tiny electrodes on her tongue. To her surprise, she was able to stand unassisted and remain balanced for the first time in years as her brain decoded messages from her hat and tongue (acting as an artificial balancing system). It was understandably a very emotional moment for Cheryl.

But the amazing part of Doidge's story is what happ-ened *after* the hat and plastic strip were removed. Cheryl found that there was a *residual effect*—albeit only for a short while. Each time she wore the hat, the 'learning effect' increased, to the point where an effect that initially lasted only seconds gradually built up to hours, and then days. After a year of wearing the hat on a regular basis, the learning effect was so strong that Cheryl could go months without wearing the hat. Today, she doesn't need the hat at all—her brain has completely rewired itself.

This research has beneficial implications for goal achievement. Regardless of previous results or beliefs or thoughts that occupied your mind, the brain can transform itself with the right strategies.

The ability of thoughts and beliefs to shape your life

The power of the mind to overcome severe physical and psychological problems, as discussed in the first part of this chapter, has important implications for goal setting. This is because there is clear evidence to suggest that many of the limitations to goal setting and achievement are purely imagined mental boundaries, which can be overcome if they are understood correctly and if the right strategies are employed to turn them around.

When Roger Bannister broke the record for running a mile in four minutes, sports scientists were stunned. It was deemed that the human body was not meant to be put under so much strain, and that the feat was impossible to achieve. Within three years, over 300 others had run the mile in under four minutes too. What had changed? Only the mindset and belief that something could be done.

> All personal breakthroughs begin with
> a change in beliefs.
>
> —Anthony Robbins

Similarly, we are all conditioned to believe certain things about ourselves from an early age. In fact, our core beliefs about ourselves are formed before the age of seven (this early period of learning is known as the imprint period). It is sad when limiting beliefs stay with us our entire lives based on our experiences as a child. I don't know about you, but I would prefer it if a seven year old was not responsible for the software in my mind!

So how does this conditioning affect our ability to achieve the goals we set? Well, much like the mental barriers that prevented any living human from running the four-minute mile before Bannister, our thoughts and beliefs can prevent us from achieving our goals if we are constantly thinking limiting or restricting things about ourselves and our abilities.

It is estimated that we have between 50 and 60 thousand thoughts each day. Our 'internal chatterbox' is constantly muttering away, providing a running commentary on and analysis of our everyday lives. Someone's internal chatterbox might sound like this: 'Why did she ignore me? What am I going to have for lunch? What a great day! What's in it for me? When's this chapter going to end?' (This final statement would naturally only apply if you were reading a different book!)

It is estimated that between 95 and 98 per cent of the thoughts that we have each day are the same as the ones we had the day before; we are very much habitual thinkers. The trouble with this habit-driven way of thinking lies in the number of negative thoughts we allow to infiltrate our minds. Some experts have estimated that between 70 and 80 per cent of our thoughts about ourselves are negative. When we repeat negative thoughts enough times in our minds, they become debilitating beliefs.

Beliefs are merely ideas that we are convinced are true. Some beliefs are absolute truths (such as the world being round), but many beliefs are open to interpretation based on individual experiences. Beliefs can make us incredibly happy or amazingly miserable, because they have a huge effect on our behaviour.

Beliefs form the success or failure blueprints operating in our subconscious minds, and they can have a huge impact on our ability to reach our goals. Many of our beliefs actually empower us, but some beliefs can hold us back from living fulfilling lives. They can limit our job prospects, decrease our self-esteem, increase self-doubt and sabotage our best efforts. They are often referred to as limiting beliefs.

Limiting beliefs work by creating self-fulfilling prophecies that can hold us back from achieving our true potential. For example, if you were asked to fill in the blank at the end of the sentence, 'Life is …', how would you answer it? Some common responses are listed following:

▫   life is unfair

▫   life is what you make of it

- life is beautiful

- life is hard.

If you believe life is unfair, naturally you will somehow manage to find evidence that supports that belief. It is likely that this one belief will be like a heavy weight you drag around with you everywhere you go. The weight, however, exists in your mind, and sometimes it can be hard to cut the cord, especially if you are not aware that the belief exists or that it limits you.

Following are some examples of limiting beliefs that hold many people back. See if you can identify with any of them.

- I'm not clever enough.

- I'm too old or too young.

- Being overweight is in my genes.

- I will only fail and then feel lousy.

- I'm boring.

- I'm ugly.

- If I succeed then I'll have to change the way my life is now.

- I've never been lucky.

- Something awful will happen.

These are just some of the beliefs that sabotage our chances of achieving our goals. The sad thing is that sometimes we have no idea that we have these limiting beliefs operating in the background of our mind. I have met people that have had the same limiting beliefs for 20 or 30 years, and are miserable because of it. The suggestion that someone could change their belief is often met with stiff resistance, and the person with negative beliefs about himself or herself might say something like, 'I am right in what I believe—who are you to tell me what I believe is wrong?' It can be hard to let go of an old belief, but sometimes it is the best thing you can do.

In addition to creating limiting behavioural effects, negative beliefs can affect our emotional state. This is because our brain strives for harmonic thinking and is always trying to restore conflicting viewpoints into a kind of internal peace. It does this by discarding information that contradicts a belief that we have about ourselves, even if there is mounting evidence that refutes the belief.

Table 10.1 demonstrates the way in which some of these limiting beliefs affect our emotional states together with our actions.

Table 10.1: effect of limiting beliefs on behaviour and emotion

Belief	Actions	Possible emotional consequences
Everyone must love and appre- ciate me.	• Try to please everyone and often end up pleasing no-one • Unassertive behaviour	• Low self- esteem • Anxiety • Depression
People should have the same values as I do.	• Try to change others • Hold resentment towards others who do not share values	• Anger • Frustration • Depression • Resentment

Table 10.1 *(cont'd)*: effect of limiting beliefs on behaviour and emotion

Belief	Actions	Possible emotional consequences
'If it isn't broken, don't fix it' belief	• Avoid dealing with problems and potential problems, which leads to them only getting much worse	• Guilt • Depression • Discontent • Lack of passion • Relationship tension • Feeling of helplessness

Knowing the link between our beliefs, actions and emotional responses is important if we are to understand what our beliefs are. Once you know your beliefs, and the consequences of acting on them, you can then decide whether you want to keep them or not. By keeping limiting beliefs, you choose to allow your limiting actions and emotional responses to continue unchecked.

Choose to be free of these, and make a concerted effort to work out and implement the steps towards achieving your goals. Your life results will improve dramatically.

You *can* replace your negative beliefs with positive ones, and this can have an amazing impact on your ability to reach your goals. To realise our true potential, we must be very careful as to what we allow ourselves to think and believe. Replace the negative beliefs about yourself with positive ones, and look for evidence to support these new positive beliefs. Some examples of positive beliefs are described following:

- I have unlimited potential.

- I am intelligent.

- I am a good person.

- I am happy with who I am.

- If things in my life aren't working, I can take steps to put things right immediately.

- I am comfortable with my appearance.

- I believe I can do anything I put my mind to.

- My life has a great purpose.

- Life is an amazing adventure.

- I am responsible for my life.

> I knew I was going to be a comedian when I was about six. You get what you believe you'll get.
>
> —Billy Connolly

If you believe that you won't achieve your goals, you probably won't. However, if you are able to nurture some empowering beliefs and then back them up with experiences that support that belief, you are well on your way to achieving your target.

Getting a magic mindset

The magic mindset is where you have total belief in your skills, knowledge and ability to take you to a solution. You have the mindset to deal with the challenges you might face in a positive and empowering way. It is the mindset of champions which unfortunately too few people possess; it knows no boundaries.

Most people tend to be just fine when the birds are singing, the sun is shining and prospects are good — but when things don't go exactly to plan, our mindset is tested. It is our ability to deal with difficult situations that can make all the difference when it comes to achieving our goals. People who have a magic mindset are able to stay calm under pressure and focus on the solution rather than the problem; the truth is that they tend to respond better to life's challenges and, for the most part, they get better results because of it.

Every day holds the potential for difficult situations: the train might be late; the car might not start; your phone bill might be too high; you might get abducted by aliens … okay, so the last one is unlikely. But with the occurrence of each situation, you have a choice about how to respond. You can't always change the situation or incident, but you can always change your response. By choosing a better response, you change the resulting outcome; and it makes sense that positive responses are more likely to give you a favourable outcome.

Blake's TIP Situation + Response = Outcome.

Following is a hypothetical example of how two different people might handle the same situation.

> *Situation:* Dave and Jim are both late for work because of a traffic jam.
>
> *Dave's response:* Dave becomes stressed, angry and experiences road rage.
>
> *Jim's response:* Jim leaves a message at work and just enjoys listening to some good music — there is nothing that Jim can do about the traffic so why stress about it!
>
> *Dave's outcome:* Dave is frustrated for the whole day and is unpleasant to be around.
>
> *Jim's outcome:* Jim feels refreshed at work and performs at his usual high standard.

If both Dave and Jim had a goal to get a promotion, you can see how their responses to difficult situations could play a key role in that decision. Dave might behave himself out of a promotion because of his tendency to respond poorly to stressful situations.

> It's not what happens to you that counts. It's what you do about it.
>
> —W Mitchell

The greatest power you possess is the power to choose. You get to choose what you think and how to best respond to any situation. By choosing empowering responses, you are able to maintain a magic mindset that will help you achieve your goals.

The key to making the best choices when responding to a negative situation is to focus on the outcome that you want to achieve, and then respond according to that. Too many people don't think enough about the outcome; they *react* rather than *respond* to situations—and then wonder why they don't achieve their goals!

A person with a magic mindset experiences an array of emotions from day to day, just like anyone else. But there is one difference: the emotions or feelings experienced will tend to be much more positive, starting from the moment the person gets out of bed in the morning. These positive, empowering feelings tend to remain throughout the day, despite setbacks and disappointments.

So how do you get a magic mindset?

The magic mindset for goal achievement has the following critical ingredients:

- commitment to choosing an empowering response to each situation that occurs

- a mind full of empowering beliefs, and a willingness to shed limiting ones that aren't consistent with the results you are looking for

- a high percentage of positive thoughts, feelings and actions each day

- courage to step outside your comfort zone and think in new ways

- a strong focus on what you want and a commitment to getting there.

The remainder of the chapter will explain in simple and practical terms what you can do to achieve this.

The belief-changing blueprint

Frederick Lehrman likens the mind to an old building inhabited by long-term tenants. The tenants have been managed by the same landlord for many years. When we decide to change, it's as if a new landlord has come in and informed the tenants that it is time to change, and this will result in an increase in rent. Most tenants will reject the changes and want to keep the status quo — even if the changes mean a better building. Sometimes our 'tenants' are forceful and insistent that we give in to them, which can prevent us from changing our beliefs because it all seems a bit too hard.

> All right brain, you don't like me and I don't like you. But let's do this, and then I can get back to killing you with beer.
>
> —Homer Simpson

Changing our belief system can be very challenging, but at the same time it can bring with it some awesome rewards (including helping us achieve our goals). So how do we shed limiting beliefs for good? There are five steps that can help you change your beliefs for the better, which are discussed following.

1 Question the accuracy of your existing beliefs

If a belief is a feeling of certainty about something, you need to shake up the limiting belief to create doubt around it. For example, if you wanted to get rid of the belief that you 'can't lose weight', you might start by looking at examples of others of a similar age who have transformed their bodies and lost weight. You might even cast your mind back to times when you have lost weight in the past—thus disproving the theory that you can't lose weight.

2 Pinpoint a more empowering belief

Out with the old, in with the new! To rid yourself of a belief that is not working for you, you must replace it with one that does work. The trick is deciding on the most empowering belief. As all beliefs are stored in the subconscious mind, we need a bridging belief to aid in the transition into the subconscious. A bridging belief is an interim belief that is better accepted by your subconscious mind. Here is an example of a lady I worked with by the name of Susan:

> *Limiting belief:* I can't perform at job interviews. (Susan's belief was so strong that she actually fainted at interviews from the fear that engulfed her mind.)
> *Bridging empowering belief:* I am becoming more confident in my ability to perform well in job interviews.
> *Empowering belief:* I am highly competent at job interviews.

Susan had been unemployed for over eight years and desperately wanted to change her limiting belief. She was successful at a job interview a week after I worked with her. It was wonderful to see her shed a belief that had been causing her so much pain.

3 Adjust the pain/pleasure paradigm

Now you need to utilise the twin forces of pain and pleasure in the mind. Think about the pain that will occur if you *don't* change your debilitating belief. What negative emotions will you continue to feel? How will the limiting beliefs hinder your relationships? How will the beliefs sabotage your goals? At the other end of the spectrum, how will the new, empowering belief make a positive change in your life?

4 Recondition your subconscious with positive thinking

To implant an empowering belief, you must replace the thoughts that fuel your limiting belief with empowering ones to fuel a new, positive belief. If you combine the process of replacing negative beliefs about yourself with empowering ones that have some positive emotional intensity, the effect of the process will be enhanced. I refer to this as emotive thoughts infusion (ETI) and it has a powerful effect on changing core beliefs faster.

So how do you do it?

The parts of the day closest to sleep—first thing in the morning and last thing at night—are the two most beneficial times to do the emotive thoughts infusion. The process of emotive thoughts infusion involves telling yourself the empowering belief you've decided on while *infusing it with positive emotion*. That way, the positive belief becomes lodged into your subconscious mind. Susan pictured herself being confident and relaxed in an interview context, and she felt good about it. She did not let her mind spiral into negative thoughts. She took control of her mind, something we can all do with practice and commitment.

5 Create experiences that support the new belief

If the emotive thoughts infusion is the flame, the experiences that follow are the firewood. Experiences enable the 'change fire' to stay alight. Susan practised mock interviews with friends and relatives, as well as learning some techniques to help her with her confidence. These experiences fortified her belief in herself, gave her much-needed confidence and improved her interview skills. The smile on Susan's face when she gained employment after eight years of trying is something I will never forget!

The formula for shedding limiting beliefs really works. It takes some time and energy each day, but it is well worth the effort. New, better beliefs can be the kick-start your goals need.

Avoid sinking into sameness

Having positive, empowering beliefs stored in the subconscious mind is critical to help you achieve your goals, but even people with a plethora of strong beliefs at their disposal can become stuck in a rut. They lose energy and drive because they feel chained to routines that allow for little growth, which slowly pulls them down and makes it harder to maintain the energy needed to pursue and achieve goals.

Getting into certain routines and patterns with the way you live your life can yield some great results ... for a while, anyway. The danger lies in becoming bored, apathetic and tired because the element of surprise and spontaneity has been lost. Feeling like that won't give you the impetus and energy to plan and achieve your goals.

Remember the first date you went on with that someone special? You were probably a little nervous, and you may have spent a lot of time working out what to wear and choosing the venue; you probably made a real effort to impress your new love interest. Fast-forward 20 years: you go out to dinner at the same place you usually go; you wear the same clothes you usually wear; and you can pretty much finish your partner's sentence. It might be comfortable, but is it too constricting or claustrophobic? Is 'sinking into sameness' bad for the process of achieving our goals?

If we repeat the same routines for a long period of time, our mind becomes lazy. This can affect our energy levels, which need to be high to give our goals the proper attention they deserve.

So what do you do when you find yourself sinking into sameness?

Each year you could have a list of new experiences you'd like to have, and then schedule them in your diary. That way you are likely to keep your inner spark lit. Here are some ideas about how to avoid sinking into sameness:

▫ If you walk every morning as exercise, perhaps you could change the route so that you include a few hills or some stairs. You could wear a pedometer and time yourself to improve on your speed. Perhaps you could walk with different friends or listen to music while you walk.

▢ If you live by yourself and are in the habit of warming up frozen meals and sitting in front of the TV, you might consider going out with friends at least twice a week. Do an Italian or Thai cooking course, or join a social club that dines out occasionally.

▢ If work has become boring for you, look at ways to improve your efficiency. Change the order in which things are done. Even redecorating the office or work area can make a huge difference.

▢ If you are bored with your partner, don't throw him or her away. Communicate, do something different together, rekindle the love that was there, take an exciting holiday together or take dancing lessons!

Regardless of the situation you face, there are always ways to stimulate the senses and get your motivation mojo back.

Having a magic mindset can play a big part in achieving your goals. A magic mindset is about focus: always focus on what you want rather than on what you don't want! By focusing on empowering meanings, you can increase your resilience to life's obstacles, problems and challenges, and you can get more of what you want in life.

Conclusion

Where to from here?

If you have read this far, you are committed to making a difference in your life and are prepared to take on some new challenges to reach your goals. It has been a privilege to share the journey with you so far, and I look forward to hearing about all the amazing results you achieve in your life after applying the key messages outlined in this book.

The level of success you achieve in applying the strategies you've learnt depends entirely on you. To put the strategies into practice, you must be willing to 'take the plunge' by making a decision to follow your dreams. You must be disciplined and strategic about setting goals and employing strategies that will lead you to them. It's about making the most out of each opportunity that presents itself.

I had a personal experience of lost opportunity at the ripe old age of 11 that I'm sure you can relate to. For the end-of-school dance in year six, the teachers instructed us to take a partner to the dance. I had a huge crush on a girl by the name of Carolyn at the time, but didn't have the confidence to talk to her—let alone ask her to the dance. I was waiting for the perfect time, but it was amazing how many reasons I came up with to justify my excuse that the timing was wrong. Then, the news got around that someone else had asked her and she had accepted. I missed my chance, and ended up going with the tallest girl in the year because I had left my run too late (I wasn't exactly tall at the time, so we looked very odd together!). I missed out on my opportunity back then, but that wasn't the only one I missed. Indeed, there have been many opportunities that I have talked myself out of pursuing over the years, whether out of fear, self-doubt or uncertainty.

Missed opportunities hold many of us back from achieving our goals and dreams. We can't change the past, but we can choose to make the most of each opportunity that presents itself from now on.

The following story will help you to conceptualise the mental shift you'll need to undertake in order to successfully implement the strategies you've learnt in this book.

Imagine you are attempting to cut down a really big tree using an axe. Again and again you strike the tree, hoping to see an indentation forming in the trunk as a reward for all your hard work. But there is one problem: the axe is blunt. You realise that it is going to take you a long, long time to cut down that tree—assuming you even have the energy and stamina to get there at all!

On the grass behind you is a fully functional chainsaw. You could just reach over and use the chainsaw to cut the tree; it would only take you a few minutes, and the job would be done quickly and painlessly. A lot of people would hesitate to use the chainsaw, preferring instead to whittle away slowly and unproductively with the blunt axe. The chainsaw causes anxiety because it is different from what people are used to: it's more powerful, but it has a higher perceived chance of injury. People *know* how to use the axe; using a chainsaw is outside their comfort zone.

The same principle applies to goal achievement. You have been given some powerful tools to take you to your goal faster, but it can take effort and some acclimatisation to take full advantage of the techniques. We are creatures of habit, so when it comes to replacing old habits with new and better ones there will be some internal resistance from our subconscious, which may attempt to thwart our progress. The key is to stay vigilant and focused.

By setting goals and taking action based on well-thought-out plans, you can achieve anything you put your heart and mind to. Don't sell yourself short; you have amazing gifts at your disposal. It would be such a shame if you didn't share your talents with the world.

To assist you further, I have uploaded more than 70 free articles to my website. The content includes the very best inspiring quotes and a free online personal assessment, which will give you instant feedback based on your results. There is also my free monthly e-newsletter, *Momentum*, which will help you continue your journey towards reaching your goals and real success. The URL is <www.blakebeattie.com>.

Remember that while reaching meaningful goals is a wonderful experience, it is not necessarily the end results that are most important. The real achievements can be measured in terms of the lessons we learn along the way; the challenges we overcome; the confidence we build; the skills we acquire and the personality traits we develop, all of which enable us to realise some of our enormous potential.

I sincerely hope by applying the principles talked about in this book, you will benefit for many years to come.

> Twenty years from now you will be more disappointed by the things that you didn't do than by the ones you did do. So throw off the bowlines. Sail away from the safe harbor. Catch the trade winds in your sails. Explore. Dream. Discover.
>
> —Mark Twain

Appendix

Goal-achievement time line exercise

This appendix is designed to help you entrench your goals into your subconscious mind using the goal-achievement time line exercise.

First, fill in the time line provided on page 232 by filling in the significant events that have happened in your life. Real events from your personal history should be filled into the historical part of the time line (all the things that happened before your current age). In the 'future' part of the time line, you should include events that signify the completion of goals you have set for yourself, and the events leading up to them. For example, if you are 30 years old, you might include such events as 'first day of primary school' in the 6 to 10 year age bracket, or 'first kiss' in the 16 to 20 year age bracket. Then, if your goal is, for example, to have lost 10 kilograms by the time you are 35, you'd write that goal in the 31 to 35 section.

Age	Significant events
0 to 5	
6 to 10	
11 to 15	
16 to 20	
21 to 25	
26 to 30	
31 to 35	
36 to 40	
41 to 45	
46 to 50	
51 to 55	
56 to 60	
61 to 65	
66+	

Next, entrench the goals you'd like to achieve into your subconscious using the script opposite. To achieve the optimal mental state for this exercise, you'll need to relax your mind in whatever way works best for you: you might play relaxing music, meditate, have a bath or relax on the sofa. Minimise distractions and have no major 'to-do' item playing on your mind.

Then, either read the script below or have someone read it to you.

In a moment, what I need you to do is close your eyes. You are going to float above the place where you are sitting at this very moment.

While floating above your body, I want you to look down and see your life's time line rolling out below you. You can see the time line drift off into the past and into the future.

I want you to float back along your time line to the moment you were born. From there, slowly move along your time line and notice all the significant events of your life. Visualise the events that happened to you when you were a toddler, through primary and high school and up until the present day. Take a few moments to fly above your time line, so you can see down into the significant events that have happened in your life.

Now, when you are ready, I want you to fly back along your time line to this present moment. You should be seeing yourself sitting down listening to this.

Look back along your time line to all the events that have happened in your past. Now, turn around to see your future time line. There are some wonderful things that are going to happen in your future. I want you to turn your attention to the goal you really want to achieve, and the date you want to achieve that goal. This time, I want you to fly into the future, high above your time line.

Now I want you to hold that goal in your hands and gradually put your goal into the time line. Fly above the moment your goal is achieved in your life. Can you see it? Now I want you to float down into the exact moment that you achieve that goal. I want you to take in that moment very carefully: see what you will see, hear what you will hear and feel the feelings that you will feel. Congratulations. You have achieved your goal.

Now, double the intensity of your feelings by focusing even more carefully on the achievement of your goal and infusing feelings of happiness, satisfaction and pride.

When you are ready, I'd like you to float out of that future memory so you are looking down on it once more. Good. Now, from that position, I want you to look along your time line again and notice all the steps being completed between now and the moment you achieve your goal. They are all fitting nicely into your time line, right up until you achieve your goal. Excellent! Once all the steps have been implanted nicely into your time line, I want you to fly back along your time line once more and return to the present day. When you are ready, fly back down into your body. Good.

When you are ready, open your eyes and return to the present. You have now implanted your goal into your time line.

This is a powerful tool which should be repeated regularly for optimum entrenchment. With every repetition, you will notice clearer, stronger pictures of the achievement of your goals, which will cement the goal into your subconscious mind. With visualisation and time line therapy, there will no longer be any case of 'could do', or 'should do', or 'like to do'; it will be a case of being happy that you have achieved so much.

Index

accountability buddies 109, 203
addiction 137–139, 144–145
advisers 127
age 60–61, 99, 157, 214
Ali, Muhammad 162
Althusuler, Michael 80
antidepressant medication 31–32
Aristotle 132
Armstrong, Lance 84–85, 101
athletes 14, 59, 153
   —visualisation techniques and
     156–157, 203
attitudes 12–16, 82–85, 103–104
awareness
   —opportunities and 58
   —problems with 49, 94–95,
     100–103, 113, 133, 139, 202
   —values and 34

balance 18–19, 32–43, 52–53
   —diet and 106, 140
   —shifting out of 46–48
Bannister, Roger 211–212
Beatles, The 101

Beattie, Clinton 24–25, 53–55, 156
Beckham, David 157
beliefs 77–79, 211–217
   —changing blueprint 207,
     221–224
   —empowering 217, 220–224
   —habits and 145–146
   —in self 110
   —negative 135, 215–216, 223
   —placebo effect and 208–209
Bennett, Bo 158
Boldt, Laurence G 121
brain 208–211, 215
   —habit and 149–150
   —reticular activating system
     and 72
   —rewiring 72
   —state 163
   —visualisation and 157–158
Brain That Changes Itself, The
   155–156, 210
Branson, Richard 84
Brown, H Jackson Jr 81
Buffett, Warren 137

Canfield, Jack 76
careers 37–38, 40–41, 45–48, 51, 60, 64
Caroll, Lewis 29
Carrey, Jim 81
challenges, overcoming 39–40, 53, 83, 127, 188, 218, 230
Christie, Linford 157
Cleese, John 2
Clinton, Bill 4
Cole, Edwin Louis 127
comfort zone 15, 22, 117–120, 123, 220, 229
—transition 119
compounding return, law of 106–107
Connolly, Billy 1–2, 217
Cool Runnings 109–110
Cosby, Bill 20
Covey, Dr Stephen 193

da Vinci, Leonardo 29
deadlines 80, 94, 175, 189, see also time lines
death 29, 75, 192
—fear of 114
defining moments 26–28
delegating tasks 189, 196
diaries 53, 73, 147, 164, 170, 225
diet 79, 105, 106, 140, 199
—industry 149, see also weight loss
direction 21, 30, 33–34, 43, 49, 124
disappointments 12–14, 113, 220
—attitude to 101–102
discipline 3, 90, 98, 104–109
Disney, Walt 156
distractions 83, 94, 126, 163, 233
divorce 31, 38
Doidge, Dr Norman 155, 210–211
doubt 78, 161, 164, 175, 222
—self-doubt 11, 78, 91, 109–112, 115, 213, 228
dreams 1–4, 6–7, 11, 15–16, 29, 162, 207, 227
—goals and 80–81, 89, 228

—habits and 131
—living other people's 71

eating 108, 134, 138, 144, 148–149, 199, see also weight loss
Edison, Thomas 101, 123
Einstein, Albert 81, 84
elasticity 74–75
energy 37–41, 51–52, 83–84, 87, 194–196, 199–202
—toxic 175
entrenchment 135–136
—habit entrenchment model 136–138, 234
excuses 4, 16, 90, 95–100, 109, 203

FIVESTAR model of momentum 193–206
Ford, Henry 2, 78
Foreman, George 60–61
four pillars of habit shift 142–150
Frankl, Victor 81–28
friends
—as advisers 9–10, 28, 142, 197
—as supporters 70, 126–127, 175–176, 181, 226
—connection with 40–41, 44, 48, 51
—loss of 114
fulfilment 4–6, 30, 46, 166, 213

gambling 137, 148
Gandhi, Mohandas 15
goals 4–6
—achievement of 158–160, 167
—attitude to 103–104
—barriers to achievement of 121–122, 129–130, 131
—brain and 63
—career and 37
—last day legacy and 28
—magic mindset and 220
—neuroplasticity and 210–211
—placebo effect and 208–209

—POWERTIP 57–59, 67
—rewards for reaching 205–206
—self-doubt and 109–113
—time lines and 65–66, 80
—tracking progress of 42, 195, 203–204
—unsatisfying 18–21
—visualisation techniques and 154–167, 231–234
Goldberg, Whoopi 6
GPS navigation system 34
Graybiel, Ann 149
Gretzky, Wayne 11

habits 92–93, 98–109, 131–136
—action steps to break 148–149
—entrenchment model 136–139
—four pillars of habit shift 142–150
—habitual thinking 213
—payoffs for 143–147, 150
—personal 140–141
—positive habit change action steps 148–149
—reason to change bad 145
—relapse 149–150
—seven habit shift essentials 150–151
—shifting 139–145
—work 141–142
health 36–41, 51–52, 79, 109, 115, 148, 200
—nutrition and 199
—problems with 32, 97, 117, 133, 143, 156, 193
—weight loss and 44, 78–79, 86, 146, 180, 188, 196, 200, 206, 222
Hillary, Sir Edmund 130
Hillel 58
Hill, Napoleon 80
Hoffer, Eric 39

illness 11–12, 75, 96, *see also* health
—fear of 114

imprinting 154, 158, 162–163
injury 11–12
inspiration 174–175, 194, 197–198

Jeffers, Susan 116
Jenner, Bruce 72
Joel, Billy 6–7
Jolie, Angelina 21–22
Jordan, Michael 125

Kasparov, Garry 155
Kaye, Danny 23
Keller, Helen 81, 84, 199
key learning areas 177–179
key performance indicators 71
King, Martin Luther Jr 15, 84

last day legacy 28–29
lateral thinking 98, 179, *see also* power plan
law of compounding return 106–107
laziness 75, 144
learning 18, 37–39, 181
—zone 120–121
leisure, *see* recreation
life balance 18, 38–39
life-centric assessment wheel 41–43, 46
life-centric wheel of life 37–39, 42
life purpose 18–19, 26, 30, 34, 38, *see also* values, meaning of life
limiting beliefs 212–216, 221–224

magic mindset 207–209, 218–220, 226
Maltz, Dr Maxwell 110
Mandela, Nelson 15
marathons 13–14, 98–99, 204
Marx, Groucho 20
Mays, Benjamin 63
meaning of life 17–21, *see also* success, values
mediocrity 110
Michelangelo 81, 156

milestones 148, 169–170, 198, 205
mind map 183
mindset 104, 112, 145–146, 175, 188
   —magic mindset 207–209, 218–220, 226
mini goals 198
mission statement 20
mistakes 26, 151
   —fear of 114
   —learning from 119–120, 123–124, 128
Mitchell, W 219
momentum 70, 81, 91, 94, 171, 178, 189, 191–195, 205–206, *see also* motivation
   —FIVESTAR model of momentum 193–206
   —four quadrant model of momentum 185–187
money 15, 22, 39–40, 45, 49, 51–53, 95, 106, 159, *see also* resources
Mother Teresa 15, 81, 84
motivation 191–193, 205, 226
   —achieving goals and 83–85
   —mood and 200
   —speakers and 197–198
   —prioritisation and 187–188
   —visualisation and 153–156, 160–161
Mount Everest 130, 153, 159
music 36, 64, 94, 104, 163, 183, 219, 226, 232
National Centre for Refugee and Immigrant Children 22
Neeson, Liam 22–23
negative beliefs 135, 215–216, 223
neglected life areas 47
neuroplasticity 208, 210–211
nutrition 199

Obama, Barack 15
O'Brien, Dan 73

obstacle override technique 129–130
Olympic Games 12–13, 60, 72, 153, 157
opportunity 26, 57–62
oracles 127
ownership 69–70

pain/pleasure paradigm 121, 136, 223
Parton, Dolly 126
Pausch, Randy 10–11
Pay it Forward 61
Pay it Forward Day 62–63, 76
payoffs (for bad habits) 143–147, 150
performance 90, 94, 100, 111, 156, 157, 189
pessimism 90, 101–104
Phelps, Michael 153
placebo effect 208–209
plans 4, 16, 90, 169–172, 189, 191, 204–205, *see also* triple P effectiveness blueprint
   —action 171, 179
   —consequences of badly organised 172–173
   —power plan 170–174, 184, 189
Plato 17
positive habit change action steps 148–149
positivity 85–87, 103–104, 112, 122–123
power plan 170–174, 184, 189
power play 170–171, 181–184, 189
POWERTIP 57, 65–88
precision 66, 68–69
pre-habit 132–135, 138
priorities 97, 171–172, 184–185, 189
   —procrastination and 75, 92
   —values and 48–53, 64
procrastination 75, 90–94, 138, 144, 148

Psycho-Cybernetics 110
Psychology of Winning, The 86
purpose 18–23, 26, 30, 32, *see also* values, meaning of life

quotes (for inspiration) 194, 197, 198, 229

Rand, Ayn 26
RAS, *see* reticular activating system
reality check 22–26
recreation 37–38, 41–42, 45–48, 51, 64, 200
Reeve, Christopher 85
relapse 149–150, *see also* habits
relaxation 45, 144, 200, 224, 232
—of the mind for visualisation 163–164, 166, 198
—music and 183, 232
resilience 91, 124–127
—empowering beliefs and 226–227
resources 170–174, 178–179, *see also* money
—excuses and 95, 99
—prioritising 51
reticular activating system 71–72
review systems 67, 107–108, 130, 138, 195, 204
rewards 94, 109, 148, 151, 194–195, 203, 205–206
risk 116–119, *see also* comfort zone
roadblocks of underachievers 96–97
Robbins, Anthony 49, 212
Rohn, Jim 105
routine 23, 224–225
Rowling, JK 101

satisfaction 41–46, 49, 162
—career and 40
Saville, Jane 12–13
Schultz, Cheryl 210–211
Schwarzenegger, Arnold 153
Seinfeld, Jerry 109

self–doubt 11, 78, 91, 109–112, 115, 213, 228
Semco 182–183
Semler, Ricardo 182–183
setbacks, overcoming 11–12, 124, 158, 220
Seuss, Dr 16
seven habit shift essentials 150–151
Seven Habits of Highly Effective People, The 193
seven saboteurs of success 89–91
Sharansky, Natan 155
Shaw, George Bernard 160
Smith, Will 16
smoking 133–134, 137
—habits and 143
—health implications of 133–134
—partners and 70
—perceived payoffs for 144
—quitting 146–147, 149, 155–156
—social 138
—triggers for 134
—visualisation and 155–156
soccer 156–157
spirituality 40
sport 45, 59, 156, 203–204
—visualisation in 156–157 203–204
strategic thinking 169–174, 182, *see also* triple P effectiveness blueprint
subconscious 34, 58, 62, 71–73, 77, 85–87, 210
—beliefs and 213
—habits and 131–139
—implanting goals into 153–158, 162–167
success 18–22, 123,
—athletes and 59–60
—barriers to 129–130
—formula for 32–34, 66–67, 169
—risk-taking and 118–119
—saboteurs of 89–91, 139

super-stretch goal 76–77
support 203
—family 51, 87, 95, 126–128,
151, 175, 195
Sydney Olympic Games 12–13

talents 8–10, 229, 105, 184, 229
tenacity 185–186, 188
thoughts 111–112, 210–215,
—controlling 93–94, 121, 196,
201, 223
—negative 101–102, 222–223
—positive 112, 150, 220
timeframes 94, 130, 170, 179
time lines 65
—technique 165–167, 231–234
timetables 53, 79–81
treadmill of life 23–25
triangle of fear 113–115
triggers, see also habits 134–135,
146–147, 149, 150
triple P effectiveness blueprint
169–172, 189
Twain, Mark 230
Tzu, Lao 36

underachievers 95–96

values 23, 26, 32, 34–35, 42, 48,
64–65, 185
—businesses 20
—priorities versus 48–53

vision posters 164–165
visualisation 153–159, 194, 198,
234, see also time line
technique
vivid visualisation technique
162–164, 167

Waitley, Denis 86
Washington, George 98
Waugh, Stephen 102–103
wealth, see also money 18–19, 115,
117
—success and 21–22
weight loss 44, 78–79, 86, 146,
180, 188, 196, 200, 206, 222
WIIFM 82
Williams, Robin 5
willpower 3
Winfrey, Oprah 84
winning
—attitude 13–15
—gold medals 12, 60, 72–73,
153, 157
—limitations of 12–15
—the lottery 70
Woods, Tiger 105
work, see careers
World Health Organisation 134
World Heavyweight Championship
60–61